DATE LABEL AT BACK

ANTHOLOGY

For the Little Angels of Dunblane

16 tiny flowers,
    Lent not given,
To bud on Earth,
    And bloom in Heaven.

Anonymous Sun reader
Manchester

All profits go to Sun Dunblane Fund

LANG SYNE PUBLISHERS LTD.
GLASGOW

Published in 1996 by Lang Syne Publishers Ltd.
Clydeway Centre, 45 Finnieston Street, Glasgow, G3 8JU. All profits
go to the Sun Dunblane Fund. Written and contributed by the
readers of The Sun.

Origination by Newtext Composition Ltd., Glasgow.
Printed by Montgomery Litho, Glasgow.

ISBN 185217 0 23 9

Foreword

This book is dedicated to all the little angels of Dunblane whose lives were senselessly taken away in a moment of madness on March 13, 1996.

The whole world reacted in horror and anguish to the terrible events of that day. Poems and letters are still flooding in to our newspaper. Ordinary people trying to express their grief or simply their anger. Every one of them with love in their hearts for the 16 children and their teacher.

This book is a selection of those touching tributes. Every penny in profit will go to The Sun Dunblane Fund which the parents of victims have requested be given to Stirling Royal Infirmary.

I would personally like to thank the printers, publishers, and all the people who volunteered their services to produce this book. Finally, thanks to you for buying this book.

May you remember the children of Dunblane forever – Megan, Hannah, John, Joanna, Sophie, Victoria, Emma, Melissa, Charlotte, Kevin, Ross, David, Mhairi, Brett, Abigail, Emily and teacher Gwenne.

Stuart Higgins, Editor, The Sun.

Dear Sun paper

Could you please spare this Little poem for Dunblane Children.

The sun has gone down
Leaving a full sky
Above the clouds
16 little angels
Above our town
Street lamps switch on
My friends have gone
now im alone
They are calling from heaven
down to there family god
bless when I see you again.

By Emma Harrison
age 13.

Salford
Manchester

4

God's Lent Child

I'll lend you for a little while,
  A child of mine, God said,
For you to love the while they live,
  And mourn for when they're dead.

It may be six or seven years,
  Or forty-two or three,
But will you, till I call them back,
  Take care of them for me.

They'll bring their charms to gladden you,
  And should their stay be brief,
You'll always have their memories,
  As a solace for your grief.

I cannot promise they will stay,
  Since all from earth return,
But there are lessons taught below,
  I want this child to learn.

I've looked this whole world over,
  In my search for teachers true,
And from the folks that crowd life's lane
  I have chosen you.

Now will you give them all your love,
  nor think the labour vain,
Nor hate me when I come to take,
  this lent child back again?

I fancied that I heard them say,
  dear Lord thy will be done,
For all the joys thy child brings,
  the risk of grief we'll run.

We'll shelter them with tenderness,
  we'll love them while we may,
And for the happiness we've known,
  forever grateful stay.

But should the Angels come for them,
  much sooner than we've planned,
We'll brave the bitter grief that comes,
  and try to understand.

Submitted by David J. Milden
Portsmouth

Thanks to all other readers who
sent in this thoughtful poem.

HOME

When loved ones go ahead of us,
 Its hard to say "goodbye",
And in our grief and sorrow,
 We are tempted to ask why.

But they have found,
 The peace and joy,
This world can never give,
 And in God's heavenly home
Its they not we,
 Who truly live.

M.J. Gurr
Brighton

PRAY

Gentle Jesus, meek and mild,
 Look up on a little child,
Pity upon my, simplicity,
 Suffer me to come to thee,
And then Jesus himself said,
 Suffer little children to come unto me
And forbid them not,
For such is the Kingdom of Heaven.

R.B.N.
Stockton-on-Tees

No words could ever explain or stop the hurt and pain. I simply give my deepest sympathy and all my love to everyone in their grief.

Azra Harvey
Lowestoft, Suffolk

It started as a normal morning,
There was no sign, there was no warning,
A mad man walked through your school grounds,
He took the lives of those around,
He showed no shame or no sorrow,
For all the parents who will have sad tomorrows

Seventeen lives he took from others,
No more hugs from their mothers
Now they're angels in the sky,
They twinkle brightly from our eyes,
Nobody can get them back again,
In all our hearts they will always remain.

Yours Faithfully

Hannah Crisp (12)
and
Faye Crisp (10)

These are a few words of comfort to all the parents of the little children who passed away in the Dunblane horrific tragedy.

Dear little children nipped in the bud
  No grief or sorrow knew
Just sent to win their parents love
  and then to Heaven withdrew.

V.S. Dunn
Pensioner (90)
Edenbridge, Kent

CATCH HOLD

Catch hold of my hand Mum,
  like you always do,
Catch hold of my hand Mum,
  For I really need you.

Catch hold of my hand Mum,
  And take away the fear,
Catch hold of my hand Mum,
  For I love you dear.

Catch hold of my hand Mum,
  It will help to ease the pain,
Catch hold of my hand Mum,
  Your touch rids the horror of
Dunblane.

Catch hold of my hand Mum,
  Though I can't see you now,
  Catch hold of my hand Mum,
The pain has gone from my brow.

Catch hold of my hand Mum,
  For our love will never wane,
Catch hold of my hand Mum,
  God bless till we meet again.

Russell Keast
Penzance, Cornwall

Following the tragic events of last Wednesday in Dunblane, I suggested to my children that they throw away all their toy guns in respect for the victims. I was warmed by the immediate response and understanding. I later thought if every parent was to make such a suggestion to their children this could be a small but meaningful gesture for the future.

Kathy Vincent
Hungerford, Berks

Just Buds

They were like little flower buds
  Who did not live to bloom,
But God he has a garden,
  And there for you is room.

Your teacher will be with you,
  You will not be alone,
We all just say "Goodbye" to you,
  As you go to your new home.

To "Mums" and "Dads" all relatives,
  Trust him, that are in his care,
And you are ever in our thoughts,
  And also in our prayer.

June Henson
Luxborough, Somerset

Love You Miss

I am sorry for the love you miss.
  I wish I could give you a loving kiss.
Everytime I think of you
  I wish there was something I could do.
Sometimes I am ashamed to smile,
  I wondered if I should for a while,
I would come and see you if I could,
  I would, I would, I really would.
When I heard what had happened that day.
  There was only one thing I could say
that is ....
I am sorry for the love you miss.

Tegan Shields,
aged 11
Gwynedd
North Wales

Dumblane Massacre.

What happened in Dumblane?
All the misery and all the pain.

16 children 1 teacher all died,
It all came as a big surprise.

I'm very sad that all them died,
When i heard I cried and cried.

I think all guns should be banned,
And not get into evil hands.

I'll be thinking of you all the time,
As you were the victims of the crime.

By Laura Jane Beynon.

XXX

Exmouth
Devon

PATH TO HEAVEN

There's a path that leads to Heaven
  Which they will soon ascend.
There they'll meet their playmates.
  And Jesus Christ their friend.
Sleep on, sleep dear babies, your parents you'll see again.
  And walk hand in hand together down God's heavenly lane.

A Wells
Chatham, Kent

JUST REMEMBER

Just remember the happy times,
  The nappies hanging on the line,
The first word they ever said,
  The first time they climbed into your bed.

The very first steps – the very first fall,
  Remember you were there for them all.
You filled those short five years with laughter
  That you can remember for ever after.

Your memories must not be sad,
  Please try to remember the good times you had,
You loved them so much – remember each day,
  They're secure – safe and happy, though far away.

They're not alone – they're all together,
  Staying innocent children - forever and ever.

Mrs K. Dack
Eastbourne

PRAYER FOR DUNBLANE

Put your arms around them Lord,
  And hold them tight,
Tell them we love them,
  And kiss them goodnight.

Never let go Lord,
  For they were too young,
Taken from us too early,
  Before their time was done.

Sixteen little angels,
  All in Heaven above,
Watch over them Lord,
  And give them our love.

Their teacher is with them
  To guide them along,
Together forever,
  But Lord, it was wrong.

Give each one a hug Lord,
  And tell them we care,
Hold on to each one Lord,
  Untill we get there.

God bless each and every one of you.

Jacqueline Hall
Toft, Cambs

Tragedies like Lockerbie and Piper Alpha resulted in huge loss of life and our heart-felt sympathy was with the bereaved. But at least there was an explanation of sorts for those terrible events. The outrage at Dunblane, however, defies all human understanding. In the name of God, what kind of a world are we living in? This was hell on earth.

Jake Smith
London

FIRST STEPS

You watched their first step
  You watched their first smile
You wiped their first tear
  They made life worth while
Your love is always true
  It came straight from your heart
But not even wild horses
  Could keep you and them apart
You'll never stop loving them
  I know you'll never try
But all the oceans in the world
  Couldn't hold the tears you'll cry
There are many words when spoken
  That may cause to dim the eye
But the saddest word when spoken
  Is the simplest good bye.

Miss C. Moore
a 17-year-old mum
Manchester

I didn't hear about Dunblane until Thursday morning, probably about 24 hours after the tragedy. It shocked and upset me. Everything suddenly became irrelevant, all other news, even college the next day.

I cried, thinking of the evidence and the families now shattered by the ten minutes of madness. My mum gave me a big hug and we cried together.

Most people have lost someone close to them, but few can comprehend anything like this. To lose a child must be the greatest loss. A little, new person, so innocent, so loving, so dependable. A little person, part of yourself.

There is nothing that can replace what these people have lost. I think all parents gave their children an extra big hug and prayed, regardless of belief, for the Dunblane families.

Somehow tears don't seem enough. There seems nothing we can do or say, but to let all of the families know that the nation is mourning with them.

Ellen Carney
Stockport

DON'T CRY

Mummy, don't cry, I suffered no pain,
  I only wish I was with you again,
Each day I see our house,
  From the sky up above,
And watch down on you with all my love,
  And at night times, I am a star,
Shining on you, and all from a-far,
  It's so warm up here,
So free and clear,
And I know one day you and daddy will be near.

Miss L. Brown (14)
Chipping Campden, Glos.

Please convey our heartfelt sadness to the families and friends of the teacher and the children who were murdered in their school.

Your front page, Pray For Them, would have meant there was not a dry eye in the whole of the British Isles.

We can all identify with those lovely children. What a waste of lovely lives. With much sadness.

Margaret and Lionel Miles
Winchester, Hants

I am a soldier with children of my own, and like all reasonable people was appalled, sickened and upset by the events at Dunblane.

This situation could have been avoided if the pompous fools who make this country's laws had learned anything from the Michael Ryan incident at Hungerford in 1987. Apart from a few people, such as farmers and those officially appointed to control vermin, there is no justifiable reason for anybody to have any type of firearm, except in a totally controlled environment.

Even service personnel must keep their weapons in the unit armoury and they are only issued when required for use in designated areas for training or competition.

The Home Office should immediately implement a ban on all firearms from being held anywhere, other than armouries in police stations or gun clubs, and there should be a minimum ten year jail sentence, without parole, for any person caught with a firearm away from an authorised location.

Words can never express the way we feel about those lost at Dunblane. May they rest in peace.

A serving soldier
Tidworth, Garrison, Wilts

FOR THE LITTLE ANGELS
SAFE IN HEAVEN, WITH YOUR
LOVING TEACHER.
GOD BLESS YOU ALL.

I WISH I COULD TAKE YOUR
PLACE I WISH I COULD
HAVE TAKEN YOUR PAIN, FOR
I WOULD IF ONLY I COULD.
BE HAPPY LITTLE ONES
NO ONE CAN HURT YOU NOW,
YOU'LL NEVER BE FORGOTTEN
LOVE FOREVER

XXXX XX XXX XXXXXX

Vicki   SOUTHSEA,
          HANTS,

LITTLE ANGELS

One night I lay a sleeping,
　　And in a dream I saw,
A crowd of little children,
　　With their teacher and our Lord.
I rushed right over to them,
　　And hugged each one so tight,
And as I stood there crying,
　　I saw a heavenly light,
Then I saw the angels,
　　Take them by the hand,
I wanted to go with them,
　　For it was hard to understand,
As I stepped outside Heaven's door,
　　And I kissed them all goodbye,
Their little smiles I'll treasure,
　　Until the day I die.

Mrs J Ellis
Coventry

I know I can't take away all the pain for the families of the children and the family of Gwenne Mayor but writing this letter and poem stops me feeling totally useless. I haven't got any children of my own yet but me and my niece are so close, and she is four years old, only a year younger than most of the little angels who were killed and if anything ever happened to her it would break me up in pieces. May God bless you all and may He take care of your precious babes.

No one knows how hard it is, to lose someone you love,
　　Dunblane has lost their precious kids, they're up with God above.
I send my prayers to families, I send my prayers to friends,
　　Your little angels are watching you, they'll be with you till the end.

R. Senter, aged 17
Rugby, Warwickshire

WE ARE NOT THERE

Do not stand at my grave and weep,
  We are not there, we do not sleep,
We are a thousand winds that blow,
  We are the diamond glints on the snow,
We are the sunlight on ripened grain,
  We are the gentle rain.
When you awake in the morning's hush,
  We are the swift uplifting rush,
Of quiet birds in circled flight,
  We are the soft stars that shine at night,
Do not stand at my grave and cry,
  We are not there, we did not die.

From a Mum
Aldershot

I was reading the stories about Dunblane one night and felt very sad, both about the poor children but also about what the parents must be going through.
It is a terrible thing to happen and I hope this man never gets any peace for what he has done to the families and their loved ones.
Of course my love and best wishes go to all the people of Dunblane and I hope they pull together at a difficult time like this. I pray for them all.

Simon Evans
Brighton, East Sussex

As the father of a small child I was horrified to learn of the tragedy at Dunblane.

My deepest sympathy goes out to the children and families who suffered and I would appeal for everybody to write to their MP, demanding legislation to ban the domestic ownership of fire-arms and stiff penalties for those who flout these rules.
Guns are tools to kill and maim and should only be carried by security forces.
Colin Ridyard
Beaumaris, Gwynedd

THOUGHTS

If thoughts can bring you comfort,
If thoughts help to dry a tear,
If thoughts can help you know,
that there are others near,
If thoughts can make it easier,
to bear your grief, somehow,
Remember then, that our warm thoughts,
Are with you, there, right now.

From 'Somewhere in
the South-East'

I WALK BESIDE YOU

I have not left or gone away,
  I walk beside you every day,
You cannot see me with earthly eyes,
  I'm like the wind moving through the skies.
So do not let your heart be sad,
  Rejoice for me and oh be glad,
That I am free to roam the heavenly space,
  Where clouds like cobwebs lightly touch my face.
And leave me with a heart so full of joy
In knowing that my soul can never die,
  Be still and let me come so near,
That I in turn can soothe away your tears,
  And let your spirit know I am for ever near.
Our lives must for the present part,
  But time with wisdom heals the broken heart,
And gives the strength to carry on,
  Until once more we meet again,
Rejoicing in eternity.

M. Moore
Scunthorpe

SIXTEEN STARS

Sixteen angels are no more
Each one's stepped through Heaven's door,
No more to see the light of day
And all we can do is kneel and pray

The sun still shines
And the flowers bloom
But in the darkness
The sadness looms.

But in the darkness
    shining high,
Sixteen stars light up the sky.

O Lord up above,
Hold them in your tender love,
And if we forget as time goes by,
Look up,
There's sixteen stars bright in the sky.

Mrs. F. Cawdell
Nottingham

This should have been the starting of their lives - these babies of Dunblane.

We lost our first child at the age of three so we know how these poor bereaved parents are grieving and they will grieve for many years. God bless them all.

Mrs. J. Richards
Chichester, Sussex

I was filled with anger and hurt at the Dunblane tragedy. I can't imagine the pain the parents and relatives must be suffering. I have an 18-month old son who is the most precious thing in my life. I don't know what I'd do if he was taken from me. Please pass on my deepest sympathy.

Catherine Scott
Stockton-on-Tees, Cleveland

ONLY A WHISPER AWAY

My dearest sweet beloved one,
I love you so, now you're gone,
To a far, and distant space,
Where time and hardship have no place,
Oh death, you gave no time to grieve,
Though only love for you to conceive,
For you must go and I must stay,
Yet, you're only a whisper away.

Until the day, where you and I
    walk hand in hand,
Across God's blue sky, yet
    we know not the reason why,
Your bright little lives were
    over, in such a way.
We never had the chance
    to say goodbye.
Yet, you're only a whisper away.

In one quick flash your life was gone
Did God know what he had done
Although he took you
So far from me
You left us a beautiful legacy
The greatest gift God gave to man
From where the world first began,
Drift into sleep, we'll dream awa,
Knowing, you're only a whisper away.

Mrs B M Wymark
taken from the original poem
written for a very beloved son
who died tragically 10 years ago,
aged 19, on April 3, 1986

20

WE WON'T FORGET

Holy Jesus up above
Give the children all our love
We won't forget that Wednesday
The day he took the kids away.

It started out a normal day
No-one can comprehend
Who decided on that morn
The children's lives should end.

We will not, cannot, won't forget
For we can't understand
We only pray they have no pain
Now that they're in God's hand.

Little children out at play
Just another normal day
Waiting for them to come home
Now in Heaven they will roam.

That day they left home five-years-old
Their paths were straight and long
They should have had a future
Now tragically they're gone.

Love and prayers, all our thoughts
Are with their mum and dad
And all their friends and relatives
Whose hearts are very sad.

We pray they are together
So we ask you God above
Let the children re-unite
Within our walls of love.

Sadness fills our waking day
The children should be out at play
We won't forget that loving smile
Now with God they play awhile.

So God we ask you keep them safe
Hold and hug them tight
Tell them bedtime stories
And kiss them all goodnight.

Lorna Macrae
Clydebank

Just a short note on behalf of our under-10 soccer team to let the parents and people of Dunblane know how deeply we felt the terrible tragedy that took place.
Words are not much good but at least they know they are in our thoughts and prayers. We live in a small village here in the midlands of Ireland and I wouldn't like to think of such a tragedy happening here.

Frankford Football Club
Kileomac
Co. Offaly, Fare

DUNBLANE

They lived – and died
Without shame I cried
Watching in disbelief
Heartbroken parents grief
A pervert decreed they die
Evil personified – please God why?
A nation weeps
As like Aberfan
For tiny babes
Life over before it began
Can't take it in
Little angels without sin
Bereavement of loved ones
We'll try to share
For daughters and sons
No longer there
The guilty will legislate
When its too late
We will always remember
United in grief
May God watch over you
Sleep little children – sleep in peace.

James Alexander Thomson
The Possil Bard
Glasgow

I am deeply saddened, like the rest of the country. I feel it's time we pulled together to do something to protect our children.
The abused, the homeless, the orphans – the list is endless. My idea is to raise money with the power of music.
Bob Geldof did it for the Ethiopians. Why can't the best of British bands pull together to save our children?

Paul Deakin
Kingstanding, West Midlands

A DUNBLANE EPITAPH

Don't cry for me now I have died
For I'm still here I'm at your side
My body has gone my soul is still here
Please don't shed another tear
For I'm still here I'm all around
Only my body lies in the ground
I am the snowflake that kisses your nose
I am the frost that nips your toes
I am the sun bringing you light
I am the star shining so bright
I am the rain refreshing the earth
I am the laughter I am the mirth
I am the bird up in the sky
I am the laughter I am the mirth
I am the cloud that's drifting by
I am the thoughts inside your head
While I'm still there I can't be dead.

John Longstaff
Richmond, North Yorkshire

On Wednesday the 13th, I listened to the reports of the Dunblane horrors, and although I was choked, I managed to contain my tears. My five year old niece came home from school at 4 o'clock, absolutely heartbroken, with her shoulders jumping up and down, and I gave her a kiss and a cuddle, and questioned, what's wrong? And why were her and mummy so late coming home from school. In uncontrollable sobs she told me she'd lost her tiny teddy bear and her and mummy were searching for it in the playground. I comforted her the best I could while she sobbed. She was worried that her tiny teddy would be frightened, lonely and cold, because he's only wearing a short sleeved jumper, and would be looking all over for her. It was then I went to the bathroom, locked the door, and my tears would not cease, because that was the type of innocence that was taken that brutal horrific morning. Like everyone else I questioned, why? and called God unprintable names, for taking babies and their teacher. I am not religious, but asked in the name of Christ, how could such cruelty be thought of and inflicted.

Miss Angela ODoherty

THE WEE POPPIES

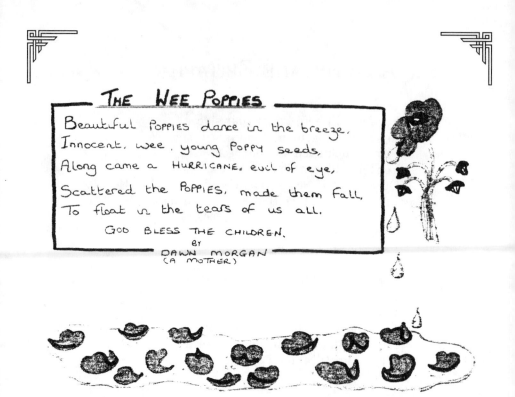

Beautiful POPPIES dance in the breeze,
Innocent, wee, young POPPY seeds,
Along came a HURRICANE, evil of eye,
Scattered the POPPIES, made them fall,
To float in the tears of us all.

GOD BLESS THE CHILDREN.

BY
DAWN MORGAN
(A MOTHER)

I cried in disbelief and sorrow for the parents who had waited outside Dunblane Primary School, hoping and praying that their child had not been slaughtered.
Sadly, for 16 sets of parents, the news every one of us dreads was all too real.
When I picked up my eight-year-old daughter that day, I could see that all the other parents were thinking the same thing: "It could so easily have been us."
When my daughter came out I cuddled and kissed her more tightly than usual.
My heart goes out to those poor parents who will never cuddle or kiss their children again.

Mrs B. Donnelly
Sheffield

HEAVEN'S SKIES

Sixteen little angels,
In Heaven's skies,
Sixteen little angels,
To soon for them to die.

Sixteen little angels,
Playing on Heaven's clouds,
Holy Angels' tears fall,
As we say their names aloud.

Sixteen little angels,
Will always be in our hearts,
Forever we will remember
That evil day,
Dunblane was torn apart.

There are sixteen new stars,
In the dark night sky,
For sixteen little angels,
To soon for them to die.

J. Porter
Kingswood, Bristol

The nation will never forget the children of Dunblane but in years to come some of us may forget when it happened.
Let us not let this happen.
We have Remembrance Sunday where we all recall those who gave their lives so that ours' could be better so let's have a day marked on the calendar for all the children and adults who have lost their lives through tragedies like Aberfan or Lockerbie as well as those who have been murdered.
Let's have this day so we can all show our respect and remember the innocent and let's call it 'Angels Day'.
And on it we should also have a minute's silence.

C.A. Riddell
Harrogate

GUARD THEM

Gentle Jesus soft and white,
  Guard those 16 little angels,
Through day and night.

Keep them warm,
  Keep them safe,
For all their parents I have faith.

But to lose someone so small
  Must be hard to bear
But now they are in Heaven
  They will be safe up there
Good night, God bless.

Stacey Harrison, aged 15
Salford, Manchester

I along with many, wept at the sadness and for the survivors. After Dunkirk in 1940 my unit was in the area from Dunblane, Braco, Greenloanings and Stanley – all in Perthshire – and we appreciated the tranquil beauty of the area, together with the kindliness of the people.

Our convoys had only to pause anywhere for a few minutes for the hospitable folk to come out with cups of tea and bites for us. Later on in the war I managed to collect a few bullets in me so I felt even closer to the children.

Old Soldier

We were very sorry to hear about the shootings in Dunblane Primary School.

Our teachers have started saying prayers in every class and at dinner times.
Not one person had a dry eye yesterday and today when we said the prayers.
The evil murderer couldn't have been in his right mind to shoot innocent schoolchildren.
We thought things like this only happen in America and Scotland was one of the safest countries in the world.
This man should have been saved so that he could be tortured by guilt and sadness at taking not just one but 17 lives.
Sixteen had hardly started.

Lisa Jamieson and Louise Coyle
*First year pupils, St Stephen's High School,
Port Glasgow, Renfrewshire*

Dear Mothers Fathers Teachers,
My heart goes out to you all I
have a young son David age 7
I know somtimes they drive you
mad, but no matter you still love
them, I know words cannot bring
your lovely children back to you
I for one have never met them
but I share my grief and tears
with you.

A Thousand times you will cry
If your Love could have saved them
they would never have died,
God must have the most beautifull
Garden

From Mrs Jean Hibberd
and Son David age 7

Bury
Lancs

For The Babes Of Dunblane

Not old, not ill, not expected to die, then why?
  Young, beautiful, everything to live for
No reason to die? then why?

Bright as the sun and flowers, shining
  Lively faces, you shouldn't die, then why?
Taken from us so soon, just settling into life
  Not ready to die, then why?

No explanation, no time for goodbye,
  Hearts so broken and the question asked...
Why, why, why did you die?

You are in our hearts and never forgotten

Anon

My thoughts hark back to that terrible Wednesday when I was working in hospital and heard the newsflash on Radio One.
I just can't stop thinking about the stricken people of Dunblane.
It's so bloody awful, I fill with tears when I read the reports and readers' letters.
It was an incredible act of evil and I can still hardly believe it.

Mr. S. Rees
Cardiff

I hope some good will come from the tragedy of Dunblane. Even if it's only that the supporters for the release of other evil child killers – like Myra Hindley – join the rest of the human race and realise where their true sympathies should lie – that's with the families, relatives and friends of the innocent victims.

Lyn Smith
Enderby, Leicester

PLEASE TELL ME

Oh Lord God bless these little children,
  Who died in Dunblane,
Our hearts are with the families,
  Who suffer the pain.
Why oh why did this have to be,
  To take them away why?
Please tell me for the hearts that are broken,
  Will they ever mend.
All we can offer is tears,
  And our deepest sympathy which we send.
And to the caring teacher who died,
  God will care for you,
And be at your side.

Karen - Dave
Essex

If we thought for one minute we could help you carry your burden we'd have already
left West Wales to be with you.
Please take comfort in the fact that the whole world grieves with you.

Elaine Rowland and Emma Bishop
Cardigan, Dyfed (parents of five-year-old children)

My name is Lianne Simone Elliot, I am 11 years old. I wrote this for all the parents and relatives of those who died.

Death, rest in peace
Unable to understand
Never ending pain
Because it hurts
Life is very precious
Always in our hearts
Never gone away
Everlasting thoughts
A very stressful time
Never-ending dreams
God Bless
Everyone feels sad
Lasting love
So innocent.

Love from Lianne
Chalkhill Estate
Wembley, Middx

FLOWERS OF DUNBLANE

They'll never feel the snow again
Nor play for hours and hours
They'll never see the baby lambs
These lovely little flowers
Their little faces that we've seen
Will always bring us pain
The tragedy of innocents
The Flowers of Dunblane.

Sheila Hamilton
Huddersfield, South Yorkshire

FOR DUNBLANE FROM WALES

Gentle Jesus, meek and mild,
Kiss them tenderly, every child,
Oh so innocent, all so true,
What they suffered to come to you.

Gentle Jesus, to you we pray,
Show them gentleness in every way,
I think of them all, my heart full of grief,
Of the sorrows to bear, whilst time was a thief.

They were our flowers, they were our sun,
Each one was happy and now they are gone,
Their fun and games was as a group,
From flowers to angels in one swift swoop.

Side by side, Lord, they walk through your gates
Always friends, always mates.

I.M. Grimaldi
Ely, Cardiff

To The Parents

The children are in Heaven,
   Getting their teacher's love and care,
And she will keep them happy,
   Till you can join them there.

Moss Sweeney
Aged 82

Sons And Daughters

I wished to write of joyful things,
   Of flowers, meadows, golden rings,
With saddened heart, my hand with pain.
   Reels at the thought of a word — Dunblane.

Once at a loss for words am I,
   These sickening scenes that horrify,
My being will not comprehend,
   The atrocity of these angels' end.

With sorrow for the 16 dead,
   Whose young lives have been so cruelly bled.
In innocence so unjustly slaughtered,
   Dunblane's sons and Dunblane's daughters.

In deepest sympathy to the parents
   Who have lives torn in two
I pray solace and some peace of mind
   May eventually touch those left behind.

I say a prayer for their teacher who,
   A mother, a wife and a daughter too,
Her aim in life to guide and defend
   A task well performed to the bitter end.

Name and address supplied

TO THE MOTHERS

We know that you are grieving,
  Your hearts are crushed and sore,
Things will never be the same for you,
  Since that tragic Wednesday morn,
We want to come and comfort you,
  And hold you oh so tight,
We want to come and tell you,
  That everything will be alright,
We want to let you know,
  That we are sending all our love,
To your darling little angels,
  In that big garden up above.
We know that words won't mean a lot,
  In your hour of grief,
We just want to let you know,
  From the bottom of our hearts,
That we all care, we really do,
  For each and everyone of you.
One day, the distant future,
  When the heartache has somehow eased,
You will look back and remember,
  How things once used to be,
Your darling little Angels,
  Laughing oh so happily.
But until then, we all know,
  That the tears will keep on falling,
And the world will still be mourning,
  For the ones you loved so dear,
We don't know why this happened,
  I guess we never will,
But there is one thing we know for sure,
  Those little ones, we won't forget,
So innocent and so pure.

Mrs Rita Baxter
Hull

32

THE TEARS

The tears for the children we never knew
  The tears for the lives that never grew
The tears for the smiles that we'll never see
  The tears for the pain and the memory
The tears for the brave who tried to save them dear
  The tears for the parents who clutch their babes near
The tears in the silence, the rivers run deep
  The tears in the toys, the pain as we weep
Words do not help the tears that we cry
  The babes, their lives, oh God why?

Kelly Mitchell
Norfolk

Having lost a daughter and a grandson at the tender age of three in both cases I, my son and daughter-in-law in Scotland can understand how the relatives of Dunblane feel.

It is beyond any parent's belief that their child should pre-decease them. Words simply cannot express the black despair into which one falls.

Let's have action to prevent such a recurrence, not platitudes.

Abolish gun clubs and their like. Only gamekeepers should be allowed guns.

There is no necessity for anyone else in Britain to possess a fire-arm. Let's have action NOW!

Francis Cooper
East Sussex

I read today The Editor's personal message. As all parents must today be in shock, you reflected every poignant point.

I would like to say something of the bravery of the poor dead teacher, Gwenne Mayor. Although the effect of this sad tragedy has not yet sunk in, I feel that this woman acted with such bravery that had she been in Her Majesty's Services, she would have received the highest award.

Before she is forgotten in the passing of time, I think that she should receive the George Cross. This will not bring her back to her family and it will not bring back the poor little souls that died at the hands of that human scum.

But it will hopefully give both her family and those bereaved some comfort to know that Dunblane will never be forgotten! She murdered no one, she didn't get £20,000 compensation for wrongful arrest, she died trying to save the lives of little innocent children.

Isn't it time we recognised these people, instead of worrying about the murderer's welfare etc?

R. Grant
Maidstone, Kent

HEARTBREAK ALL AROUND

The world is in shock with a school at Dunblane
    When a stranger walked in who was totally insane
17 were killed by the shot of a gun
    Their lives hardly used as all so young
This bizarre attack has saddened us all
    To think how a person can be so cruel
We pray for the lives that were taken away
    From family and friends on that tragic day
Safe and sound in Heaven they lie
    Always in our thoughts as we say good bye.

Miss E.J. Cairney
Folkestone, Kent

I live in the Canaries, married to a Dane and we are blessed with a beautiful daughter born in Lanzarote.

It has taken a while to write as I have been in shock since March 13th. I have read your newspaper coverage and watched the news & teletex hourly transfixed by the atrocities in Dunblane. I thought I was being dramatic until I read of mothers all over the world and especially in Great Britain experiencing the same intense feelings towards their own children, especially being the similar age to these tragic children.

I cried tears of guilt when I remembered only three days before my daughter, Kimberley, celebrating her 7th birthday, dressed as a little princess, her 21 friends all in fancy dress and a fun day had by all.

I cried tears of guilt when I thought of the mountain-bike we had bought her as a present.

Guilt, that our child was able to reach seven and their poor children who now never will.

I've never met any of these parents nor their children but feel I will never forget them. I would dearly like to make a donation to your Dunblane Fund and have found it difficult to set an amount on such a deserving fund. What I feel in my heart, so that I am never able to forget this heartbreaking time is to send the same amount as the mountain-bike cost £75, so that every time we take Kimberley out to learn to ride her bike we will remember the children of Dunblane who can now only ride their bikes in Heaven.

Please convey my deepest condolences to the families concerned by accepting my donation.

Karen Lamb
(A Geordie Lass)
Gran Canaria

NATION WEEPS

To all the people of Dunblane,
  A message from the heart,
To let you know we share your sorrow,
  Although we're miles apart.

March thirteenth, ninety-six,
  A day we'll remember forever
When sixteen innocent lives were stolen,
  And a nation wept together.

Our tears have fallen for every child,
  So suddenly snatched away,
And for their brave teacher who also died,
  On that dark and dismal day.

Our tears fall for those bereft,
  You do not bring them home,
To all the grieving mothers and fathers,
  Who have lost a daughter or a son.

We pray that some day this dark cloud will pass,
  And that you may once more see the sun,
We pray for the brothers and sisters,
  Who are missing someone they love.

May you be assured that they are all little angels
  In that playground up above,
We pray for all the relatives,
  And for the friends and neighbours too
To all in Dunblane - we can't ease your pain
  But may you know we are praying for you.

                                        Anon

35

So Much Pain

I can't believe that dreadful day,
  When all those lives were taken away,
It broke my heart, it made me weep,
  I couldn't think, I couldn't sleep.

The whole nation is still in shock,
  If only we could turn back the clock,
This tragedy has caused so much pain,
  Please God, don't let this happen again.

We're all so sad, we're all so numb,
  To see what this world has become.

Those babies families in Dunblane,
Will never be the same again,
This whole nightmare is so unfair,
And to all the families 'we do care'.

You've lost your children you dearly love,
And they are now safe in Heaven above.
You must be going through heartbreak and pain,
But one day you'll see your babies again.

Your children are in Heaven and they're all together,
And they'll stay in our hearts forever and ever.

Miss S. Hemmuth
Southend-on-Sea

THE WORLD CARES

If we could bear the burden of your sorrow, we would,
   If we could but for a minute take away your pain, we would,
If we could tell you there's a reason for this, we would.
   We'd do anything to take away your hurt.
But sometimes the road of life makes unexplained twists
   and unfortunate turns and the whole world seems
cold and heartless.
We can't tell you how sorry we are,
   That your lives have been interrupted this way
How sorry we are that we can't shelter you all from this.
   But we want you to have this message.
We are here.
   If you need to talk,
If you need to cry,
   If you can find comfort in sharing silence with us.
We are your friends.
   We are all with you.
The whole world cares.

Angela Hickey
Stanmore, Middlesex

When it came over the news that a madman had run amok killing a schoolchild and wounding others I was frozen to the spot, absolutely numbed that anyone could do such a wicked, wicked thing. Then when the full horror of it all unfolded I just couldn't stop crying. Those poor babies and their parents! That brave teacher and her family!

Surely the events of Dunblane must now mark a turning point in our society. It is time for the tide of evil to be stemmed. Time for the silent majority to stand up and fight for all that is good and right. Let that be the legacy of the Dunblane tots.

Kate Munro
York

To The People Of Dunblane

Their souls will rise up and dance with the angels,
  Their hearts and smiles will bloom with every flower in Spring,
Their laughter will echo in the blowing winds,
  Their tears will fall into the deep blue sea,
Their spirits will surround and protect children of today and
  tomorrow,
I can only imagine their parents' sorrow,
  From miles away we hear your cries,
I write this poem with tearful eyes.
  We will remember them.

Gnr. P. Mannion
17 Btt, 26 Regt. RA
Bosnia

I'm giving up the money that I earned as a football
referee last Sunday for the Dunblane Fund.

P Giblin (Gibbo)
Manchester

Broken Hearts

We never knew that morning,
  What sorrow that day would bring,
When hearts of gold stopped beating,
  And we could not do a thing.

It broke our hearts to hear of you,
  But you did not go alone,
Part of us went with you,
  That day God called you home.

Berrie Webb
Turnbridge Wells, Kent

POPPIES IN A ROW

Is God angry to make it rain?
   Why did it pour at Dunblane?
Did he want cherubs above?
   Now those angels fly as doves
Bringing hope and peace to mind,
   Underlining the wicked kind
That lies dormant in us all.
   And there a poppy will grow
In the corn, along the hedgerow
   To remind us lest we forget:
Anger and violence evil beget.
   Frustration and guns can murder bring.
How many angels do we need to hear sing
   Before we put down the guns,
Lock them up from our sons,
   Ourselves and the evil in us all?
Soon there'll be more poppies than corn
   And blazing hedgerows forlorn.
Is God not saying stop,
   Arms are too easily bought from the shop,
Beware the deadly nightshade
   To be found in everyone's glade.

Lloyd Carley-West
Dover

I cannot begin to tell you how badly I felt when I heard what happened to the class of Primary One. Since hearing it I just cannot stop crying.
I have become so very sad and depressed.
I just felt I had to write something while I cannot sleep. I just feel so helpless, shocked and angry.
How dare that man do this.

Sarah Sheila Peppiatt
Partington, Greater Manchester

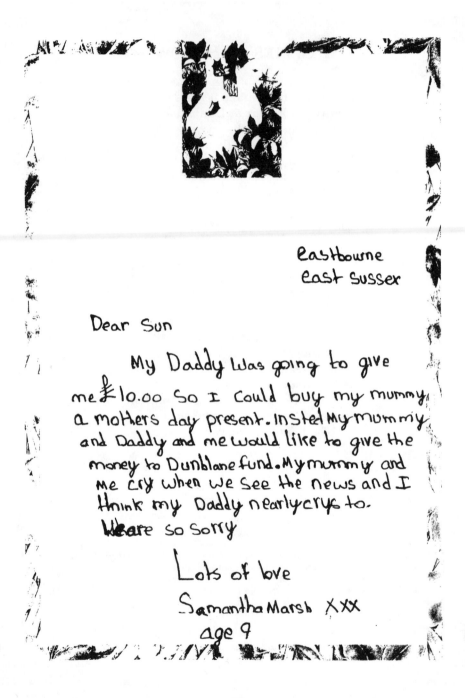

Eastbourne
East Sussex

Dear Sun

My Daddy was going to give
me £10.00 so I could buy my mummy
a mothers day present. Insted My mummy
and Daddy and me would like to give the
money to Dunblane fund. My mummy and
me cry when we see the news and I
think my Daddy nearly crys to.
We are so sorry

Lots of love
Samantha Marsh xxx
age 9

ANGELS IN HEAVEN

Mummy and Daddy please don't cry,
   We are all here safe in the sky,
Jesus is here with his arms open wide,
   We are all together side by side.

We never got to say goodbye,
   Look at the stars we will always be there,
Looking down from Heaven saying a prayer.

So mummy and daddy.
   If you are going to cry,
Just look up to the sky,
   Heaven is not so far away,
We all say goodnight till we meet again.

Meg Colpitts
Newcastle-upon-Tyne

There have been complaints about media intrusion following the tragic events at Dunblane but surely the whole world has to know what evil can do and why it must be faced and defeated. Our society is plunging into a spiritual and moral decline. The churches have lost the way and are failing to give us the necessary leadership. Could this terrible massacre be God's way of telling us that the time has come to sort out our world?

Davey Fairgrieve
Eastbourne

I am a 12-year-old girl who is very shocked about the tragedy. What kind of man would do something like this?
It feels like a piece of my heart has been ripped out even though I never knew any of the children.
Can you please give my sympathy to every one in Dunblane.

Claire Richards
Oswestry, Shropshire

A MOTHER'S LOVE

A mother's love is so precious and strong beyond belief,
  Nothing compares in depth - except perhaps a mother's grief.
She grows the seed of human life, in her body and her soul.
  Bereft of that fruit she bore,
She will never again feel whole.
  She will know the sorrow of Mary, as she watched our saviour die.
She will know the numbing pain of the echoing question "why"?
  To outlive one's child is heartbreaking,
For you know the pain is for life.
  Where once there was joy and love in your heart,
Now there is only a knife.
  A look or gesture can turn that knife, opening that aching wound
again.
  Bursting the floodgates of bitter tears, that fall like acid rain.
There are no words of comfort,
  If there were I would know what to say.
And there's nothing I can do, Except perhaps to pray.
  And I pray that God gives you the strength, to bear this unbearable
pain and hold your broken heart in his hands till it heals again.
  And in time, when mother and child are united,
In that glorious, promised land
  I pray that the Lord will have led you there gently by the hand.

C Rowlett,
Healey, Sheffield

THE INNOCENT ANGELS

Let us all grieve, let us all cry.
  Then cast your gaze up to the sky,
Sixteen bright stars shining together
  Sixteen small friends together forever.

Gone up to Heaven free from all pain,
  Now in the arms of the Lord will remain,
And one extra star shines out from the rest,
  For the teacher who gave her very best.

And the babes that are left, the ones who were spared,
  Some badly hurt, all frightened and scared,
They'll never forget the day that went wrong,
  Only love and affection will help them get strong.

But the Lord has the answer for all to see,
  Suffer little children to come unto me.

Dan Speed
Shrewsbury

It is impossible to accept or understand how any human being can do such a horrific and sickening thing as what happened at Dunblane.
This tragedy will never end for the parents who have lost their children and for the children who survived and witnessed their friends and teacher's murders. They will never be able to return to the innocence and security of childhood.
Surely after this latest tragedy the Government must take steps to ensure that schools are made secure and safe to make sure there is never a repeat of this disaster.

Sandra Fisher
Sevenoaks, Kent

OUR ANGELS

The tragedy upon that day,
  Has made the world stop still,
Our tears for those dear children,
  That took one man to kill.

Their trusting, youth and innocence,
  So cruelly snatched away,
But grieve for those they've left behind,
  For you we also pray.

Empty though your lives will be,
  Heaven will be blessed
With tiny angels, hand in hand,
  As you lay their heads to rest.

Cherish all the love they have,
  Though your hearts in two, are torn,
For every woman, man and child,
  Your loss, with you, we'll mourn.

Sleep little ones,
  Find peace.

Christine McRae
Ryde, Isle of Wight

I sometimes travel through Dunblane on my way to my home town in the Highlands. It's such a lovely quiet place and to be touched by this evil act is so unbelievable that it is heartbreaking.

As a mother of three I understand the tears that must be being shed right now. I have cried nearly every day for the victims and their families.

I see their little faces when I try to sleep at night and will no doubt see them for a long time to come.

Mrs R. Cook
Ilkeston, Derbys

TOGETHER

God must be short of Angels,
   To need those children so.
They didn't know that morning,
   It was their time to go.

We know he only loaned them
   To teach us how to smile.
But could we not have kept them,
   For just a little while?

We never will forget them,
   They're in our hearts forever.
May they find peace in Heaven,
   Until we are together.

Selina Hopkins
Lee, S.E. London

ANOTHER TOMORROW

There's always another tomorrow,
   However hard the day,
There's always an end to sorrow,
   Time wipes our tears away.

There's always a reason for living,
   Though sad your heart may be,
There's always another horizon,
   Beyond the one you see.

Sheena Russell
Wooler, Northumberland

GOD'S LAW

God's arms do not grow weary
   As he comforts your loving child,
Though he knows that you'd prefer
   To have them next to you running wild.

He will care for them and love them
   And keep them free from pain,
Knowing you will ultimately
   Meet them once again.

So cry for your child while you can,
   'till you can cry no more,
Then smile as you remember the face,
   The sound, the smell,
The happy memories you recall.

Then when you are reunited,
   You will continue life as before,
You see, there are NO GUNS in Heaven
   That's GOD'S LAW.

Janet Evans
Birmingham

D Dunblane's Babies gone to Heaven.

U United together, in our teachers care,

N Never forget us, dear Mums & Dads

B Believe we are now safe, with God.

L Loved by Him, in His Heaven.

A Always we will love you.

N Now you must all live again.

E End for us your grieving and God Bless.

Mrs F Williams
Rochdale

HARD TO HIDE

When you lose someone you love,
  The pain is hard to hide,
But when you lose their love,
  the pain goes deep inside.

Their smiles are gone forever,
  Their hands you cannot touch,
But you will never lose the feelings
  For someone loved so very much.

You'll miss them more than words can say.
  Since they were taken from you on that sad, sad day,
You'll love them till time is with you no more,
  But you will meet again of that be sure.

K. Gilfoyle
Carshalten

ONLY TIME

God only takes the special ones,
  To sit beside his throne,
He'll cherish and look after them,
  They'll never be alone.
No time for sadness, pain or fear,
  Only time for memories, laughter and a tear.

Lisa Thomas
Oxford

I saw a group of office girls sobbing uncontrollably on the train last night as they read about the Dunblane atrocity. Everyone looked so sad and grim. There was not a heart in all of Great Britain left untouched by these terrible murders – all our sympathies go to Dunblane.

A. Thomas
Guildford

Suffer The Little Children

Where have all the children gone,
    Lost for ever every one.
Slaughtered like the lambs they were,
    Murdered by a low life cur.
We tell them that all monsters are just in story books,
    That grown ups will protect them,
From murderers and crooks.
    We warn them of the stranger who may want to do them harm,
We try to keep them safe and sound, keep them well and warm.
    And then the unexpected, the nightmare, comes to life,
A community is suddenly shattered, there's grief and pain and strife.
    A throng of happy infants, innocently at their play,
When hell spewed forth the monster,
    who shattered the world this way.
In killing those little children, he took more than their young lives.
    He robbed a town of its next generation, future mothers – fathers,
husbands – wives.
Our hearts go out to their loved ones,
    to their friends and neighbours too.
We grieve with them and share their loss.
    Like them "we know not what to do".
We ask God to bless and keep them.
    Let them know they don't grieve alone.
God give them the strength to bear the weight
    of hearts as heavy as stone.

C. Rowlett
Healey, Sheffield

SKIES

Amidst a batter of snowdrops
   we weep and wonder why,
Sixteen babies and their teacher
   were singled out to die,
We struggle hard to reason,
   it seems as if we're blind,
For the answer to the question
   is lost inside a monster's mind,
The frozen masks of sorrow
   on the families left to grieve,
For forever silent angels
   who suddenly had to leave,
In this tiny Dunblane city
   amidst a mantle of trees,
A massacre of the innocents
   shocked this country to its knees,
What do you say to comfort,
   where there's grief beyond compare,
What do you say to parents,
   who's child's no longer there,
Will the sun rise on a to-morrow,
   without love they've been denied,
We can but pray together
   for the numbness to subside,
So twinkle twinkle little stars
   in the sky above Dunblane,
Spread your sun-shine on broken hearts
   to help them heal again.

Mrs. Maura T. Bye
Birmingham

DEAR DUNBLANE

March 13th 1996,
  The day innocence died
A cold, quiet morning
  Until the bullets flied.

Angel faced children
  Pure as the driven snow
About to be taken
  By the lowest of the low.

Satan in this form of man
  His masterplan is forming
Toward the school he travels
  Inner evil worming.

March 13th 1996
  I did all my crying
Seventeen wonderful people
  All dead or dying.

Sixteen little children
  Innocent and pure
A brave and caring teacher
  Of that we can be sure.

The sorrow that I feel
  The helplessness inside
The horror of the truth
  The fear of those who died.

Mothers, Fathers
  All the next of kin
All of them in pain now
  Suffering another's sin.

My prayers are for the babies
  Who died before they lived
My thoughts are with the living
  My heartfelt sympathy I give.

What a world we live in
  Politics, war and crime
All of them mean nothing
  At this most painful time.

My little boy John
  Is five years old
When he asked me "why?"
  I just felt cold.

How do you explain such evil
  To a little boy,
Who thinks guns
  Are just another toy?

March 13th 1996
  The day our children died
March 13th 1996
  The day a nation cried.

John Sullivan
Milton Keynes, Bucks

PICTURE THEM

I don't understand,
I really don't see,
How someone could harm
Kids so sweet and so wee.

Their youth taken away,
By an evil creature,
Lives of such innocent kids,
And their loving teacher.

It distresses me so,
To think of them as dead,
So I picture them as angels,
The clouds as their beds.

Each dark sparkly night,
They're tucked in by Gwenne Mayor,
A kiss and a star for each angel,
They know she does care.

God, he loves and cares for them,
Makes sure they're not sad,
Tells them soon one day,
They'll see mum & dad.

They hang their stars in the sky,
For friends and family to see,
So when they come to Heaven,
They'll know where they'll be.

V.G. (aged 14)
East London

THE SORROW OF DUNBLANE

Hearts of millions with tears like rain,
As we feel the sorrow of Dunblane,
The Angels lost but who knows why,
Such innocent souls should never have had to die,
Sorrow and hurting they left behind,
That fateful day left in our mind,
They are at peace in Heaven above,
And they can feel all our love,
Tears from God that is the rain,
How can we forget the sorrow of Dunblane.

Tears of joy amidst cries of pain,
As we remember the children and families of Dunblane,
As we sit around and weep,
Their brothers and sisters who cannot sleep,
Life must go on from day to day,
And hope the horror will fade away,
The Nation's hearts to them unfold,
Everywhere both young and old,
To record their names in the hall of fame,
So we will never forget the sorrow of Dunblane.

Sorrow fills my aching heart,
For the dear souls that had to part,
The school that was a happy place,
A dim future now has to face,
The tragedy that lives in every soul,
In their parents lives a great big hole,
The Nation's hearts are filled with pain,
For the children and the sorrow of Dunblane.

Adrian Martin
Chesterfield

THE POETRY LIBRARY

THE SILENCE

My dear ones slept quite safe last night,
With locks and love against all bane.
Not so the piteous grieving lights,
That waked the silence of Dunblane.

The meals uneaten and the games unplayed,
The beds where they'll not sleep again.
The unfinished story and the prayers unsaid –
Night fell one morning on Dunblane.

The friends I meet, the work I do –
Nothing is simple or the same.
The spears of horror pierce us through;
Part of our world is now Dunblane.

From Hungerford to Bosnia,
The footprints of the Beast are plain.
This massacre of innocents,
Has travelled far to reach Dunblane.

And each of us that sorrows now,
Has also caused unneeded pain.
We may not reach behind their shroud.
But we know this is our Dunblane.

Rip Bukeley
Oxford

To the grieving families. I offer my heartfelt sympathy and support. Treasure your memories and remember the joy and happiness your wee ones gave you. And have faith – please. One day you will meet them again.

Daisy Crawford,
Blackpool

Mrs D. Copeland

HANLEY STAFFS

Dear Editor,
          The tragedy at Dunblane
is one of the most poignant
incidents that I can remember.
Gwenne Mayor was a very brave lady,
she knew the odds were against her
when she faced the crazed gunman,
but she tried so hard to protect
her little ones, her husband and
daughters must be extremely proud of her
I personally feel she deserves a
post humous award, do other readers
agree with me?
"Jesus said "Suffer the little children
to come unto me for theirs is the
Kingdom of Heaven", may they all
rest in peace.
                    Mrs D. Copeland
                    (pensioner)

SACRIFICE

For the class primary one,
  Mrs Gwenne Mayor was number two mum,
She was loved and well known.
  Because she cared for the children like they were her own.

She loved her job and took such pride,
  It was the ultimate sacrifice for her kids, she died.

Dunblane will mourn for a woman so brave,
  In trying to protect them she was sent to her grave.

Her family will grieve for the mother and wife
  Who lived for her job and paid with her life.

Mrs L. Dodd
Southend-on-Sea

Every time I have opened my Sun over the past few days I have been unable to control my tears as the horrible, murderous result of the attack has been revealed. Why won't the Government bring back hanging?

We know this murderer shot himself but so many before are still at large and others will strike, yet, not one MP mentions the re-introduction of hanging for the murder of a human being.

To watch Dunblane again, to see the flowers strewn along the fence at the roadside, just keeps my tears flowing.

To the residents of Dunblane I offer my sympathy in this terrible tragedy. May God give all of you the courage and strength to go on.

C.J.S.
Warrington

Surely with the ever increasing tide of violent crime and associated deaths politicians must now realise that the law must undergo radical review and change particulary in regard to sentencing.

I was once in doubt concerning the death penalty but now believe it must be introduced where the case of pre-meditated and/or mass murder is involved.

Isn't it time society accepted its responsibilities and allowed the law to do its job and ensure the punishment fits the crime?

Ian Anderson
Thamesmead, London

Why Did You Do It!

Why did you do it?
   Why did you kill those little children?
You showed no sign of sensitivity
   No humanity
No conscience
   No kindness or mercy
Oh, I forgot
   You killed yourself in a gutless panic
Because you had none of those things
   Instead you were filled with evil
Anger and maybe fear
   Fear of what you had become
A lonely perverted man
   Nobody will ever forgive you
For all the pain which you have caused
   Everyone will always hate you
Why did you do it?
   Why?

Natasha Ray
Lowestoft

I had to drop you a line just to say how deeply sad I was. I would like to send my deepest sympathy and prayers to all the parents and relatives.

P. Moutrie
Wellingborough, Northants

When I took my children to school today I was actually worried for their safety. Sadly their teachers admitted they felt the same way.
They told me that the whole system was going down the drain and that things were only going to get worse.
My six-year-old daughter lost her beloved grandad recently and she asked me if the man who had hurt the children whould go to Heaven to be with him.
When I replied that he was going straight to Hell she said: "That makes me feel better. He won't be with grandad and the little children."
My heart and thoughts are with the survivors, parents and families of this truly appalling tragedy. The whole of Wales is crying with them.

Cheryl Douglas
Llanarth, Dyfed

THE LOST INNOCENCE

It's nine o'clock, the school bell rings,
   Primary year one are off to the gym,
It's their favourite lesson, it's time for some fun,
   Little did they know of the horrors to come,
They died where they fell, no time to run,
   For a monster appeared and shot them one by one,
Sixteen little lives came to an end
   Each one of them died alongside a friend,
Sixteen little angels sent to Heaven full of so much love,
   Sixteen little stars to twinkle in the sky above.

The parents came rushing up to the school,
   Hoping against hope the news wasn't true
Shouting and screaming, is my child alive?
   Hoping and praying that theirs had survived,
Then came the news sixteen had gone,
   Parents' hearts broken, a nation's hearts torn,
Sixteen sets of parents united in grief
   Each one thinking, this is beyond belief,
No more bedtime stories, no more kisses goodnight,
   No more 'mammy mammy', please turn on the light.
No more happy birthdays, no more Christmas cheer,
   All they have are memories, of the children they loved so dear.

You tried to protect them you did your best
   Not knowing how much your love for them would be put to the test.
You had to pay the ultimate price,
   This monster took away your life,
Now you rest in Heaven above,
   With sixteen angels to cherish and love,
You were their teacher and their best friend,
   Their love for you will never end.

The world is weeping with you Dunblane,
   Your tears are not in vain,
For every tear shed, will ease a little pain,
   Our hearts are full of sorrow,
What did this monster have to gain?
   By the slaying of the innocents,
In the Primary School of Dunblane.

Carole Parkin
Sunderland

INNOCENTS

Why did we lose them?
  Why did they go?
Who has the answers?
  No one seems to know.

They set off for school that day,
  With all their lives to live,
How can we understand.
  How can we forgive.

"Suffer little children
  To come unto me"
We know we need acceptance
  But it's very hard to see.

Their families have fond memories,
  Of old familiar places,
But our sweetest recollections,
  Are their little smiling faces.

Pam Turner
Wolverhampton

Ban all guns now – civilised people have no need for these weapons of destruction. I read that the killer Tom Hamilton ordered his through the post. It should not be so easy to obtain the means with which to take a life.

Paul Scott,
Liverpool

In recent times there has been much talk of breaking up the United Kingdom. Yet, in the light of the Dunblane tragedy, it has been heart-warming to see how the whole country has sympathised with an obscure Scottish town.

L. Jones
Dundee

PRECIOUS GIFT

There's 17 more stars in the sky,
   17 angels so sweet and bright,
Open the gates of Heaven for them,
   Count each one until the end.

Flowers and songs won't bring them back,
   But prayers and love will help them rest,
Take care of these angels oh Lord we pray,
   And protect their souls every day.

They were sent to you as a gift,
   These precious children so dear and sweet,
So keep them safe forever more,
   Keep 17 candles burning at night.

Keep these angels glowing,
   Rest in peace you little ones,
You'll be remembered by each and everyone,
   May God bless and keep you all.

Maggie Grostate
Sunderland

My heart goes out to the poor families who lost their children in the horror of Dunblane.

I have a daughter at primary school and you always think they are safe. But now the Government should make certain all schools are secure.

It is such a tragedy that I can't find words of comfort to remove the pain the whole world must feel.

Ban the gun clubs. Let's not give these maniacs a licence to kill.

Caroline Toner
Bellshill, Lanarkshire

How Could You?

How could you do such a thing?
   Innocent children in the gym,
Smiling faces and laughter,
   But then it turned so grim,
You opened the door and in walked evil,
   How could you do such a thing?

Primary One are in Heaven,
   Angels in the sky above,
Being looked after by their teacher, Gwenne,
   Who's giving them all so much love.

Rachel Wade
Ashford, Kent

Video nasties and their glorification of violence are distorting right from wrong. Every day on television and cinema screens thousands are violently murdered in the name of entertainment. As a society we must get back to decency and rediscover how to tell right from wrong.

Stella Parker
Nottingham

I have read so much in the last week about 'evil visiting the school' and 'where was God?' I had to find an answer. Evil did visit the school for 3 - 10 minutes, no doubt about it but God was following closely behind with love, a love that was magnified and multiplied billions of times over, a love that touched everyone in this country and throughout the world.

I wonder if we recognised God's love as the horror, grief and sorrow which united us all. But I do believe that is what it was and still is.

When the news had sunk in on that terrible Wednesday I felt so ashamed that I was a human being. How could one of my own species do such a terrible thing? In the days that followed I found that I felt quite proud and humble being a human being, proud and humble of being and feeling such deep emotions.

Although they appear to be negative emotions, they were, in fact, positive emotions of love, God's love, which we all shared.

Please give my best wishes and love in all its different forms to everyone at Dunblane school and all the people of Dunblane,

Mrs. Pauline Carroll
Surrey

Adele Louise
Woods

Dear Sir

When I heared the
news about Dunblane I was
upset so I've sent £2.00
of my Pocket money I
hope it helps

Love
from Adele
Woods from
leeds Age 11

STRENGTH

Sixteen snowdrops wilted in early spring,
  No time to spread their petals,
No time for blossoming,
  Only had a glimpse of life,
Ahead was everything.

The world in mourning,
  The evil we have to bear,
We all cry out in unison,
  Is there ANYONE up there?

May you find the strength to conquer,
  All the agony and the pain,
In all our hearts the memories,
  Forever will remain.

Kathy
Chigwell, Essex

I lost my daughter Jill so tragically three years ago so I know just how numb these poor parents must feel.
I woke up this morning, hoping to find that this was a bad nightmare just like the one I had when it happened to me.
May God bless all those little children, parents and families.

D. Bunyard
Kent

Let each of us plant a patch of snow-drops, a flower for every child. As each spring comes around and the flowers come into view, each snowy head will be in rememberance of each of you. Thus in a simple way part of you will stay.

Mrs Wright
Stoke

My heart goes out to the parents who lost their little angels. They'll never be forgotten. I speak for every mother around the world. If only we could turn the clock back.

J. A Binns
Beeston, Leeds

I wanted to share with Dunblane, to say that this has touched me in a way that will never leave me. I have just written a card to the parents of Primary One.

The tears were falling down my face as I wrote it. Tears are falling down my face still. Shocked is an inadequate description. I feel mortally wounded. How can I feel like this when it is not my own children affected by this atrocity?

If I feel like this I just cannot begin to imagine how those mums and dads must be feeling. I want to try to give them strength, to try to help them be strong.

I want to put my arms around those mums and dads, to cry with them, for them, and for the loss of their babies because that is what they were. Babies, someone's own babies.

Babies that they brought into this world and loved and cherished probably above all else in their lives, babies that they would have given their lives for.

Last night as I lay in bed I cried. I cried for the mums and dads I knew would be sitting in their baby's room that very night, holding the cherished bedtime soft toy, holding the pyjamas they had worn that very morning, laying their head where their own baby's head had lain only the night before.

The night before...when those babies were asleep, safe in their own bed, sprawled across the bed when they are asleep, when you go into their room and kiss them before you go to bed yourself and put your hand on their forehead.

You love them, you cherish them. Even when they are driving you to distraction during the day.

To lose all that. To lose your little one, your baby. The grief must be unbearable, inconsolable.

What do you do when you put their dirty breakfast bowl in the sink for the last time, pull their dirty clothes out of the linen basket, find their favourite T-shirt in the ironing?

Five years old and the light has gone, snuffed out as carelessly as the wind blows out a candle flame. No reason, no justification, nothing.

There are so many questions I want to ask. All starting with "Why?" The person that can answer one obvious answer has taken the easy way out. He should have lived so he could suffer for the rest of his mortal life.

I can only hope if there is life after death or a state of consciousness after death then Thomas Hamilton is suffering intolerably and painfully for a very long time.

The children on the other hand at rest, peacefully innocent as they were the night before sprawled across their beds as mum and dad kissed them goodnight.

I want Dunblane to know this has touched me so deeply that I will never forget.

I am sure I'm among thousands who feel the same way. You have my grief and my sympathy. I lend you all the strength I can and my thoughts are with you all,

Mrs. Suzanne Longhurst
Southampton

Anxious crowds gather as ambulances stand by.

Shocked police reveal it is the worst crime that they have ever had to face.

The ancient Cathedral of Dunblane - focal point for a shattered City's prayers and grieving.

A sad young girl reads heartrending messages on the tributes.

One sums it all up...Why?

A young lad's tribute... one of the thousands which arrived from all over the world.

Prime Minister John Major and his wife Norma arrive to pay their respects.

Crowds gather at the Cathedral for a silent vigil.

9.30am the following Sunday and Britain comes to a standstill to observe a one minute silence.

Rangers players tribute before their game later in the day against Celtic.

The tragic class and their teacher Gwenne.

73

The Queen's sorrow says it all.

Princess Anne lays flowers picked from her own garden.

Survivor Matthew Birnie, 5, pictured on a happy family holiday last year.

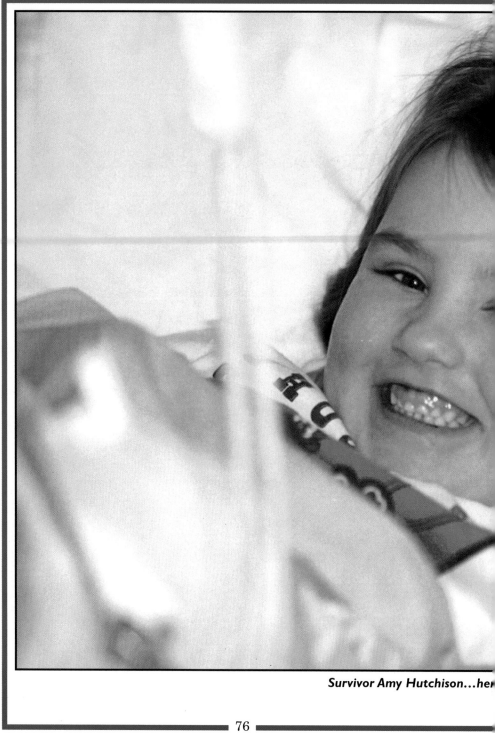

Survivor Amy Hutchison...her

gave hope back to Dunblane.

Survivor Ben Vallance who won the hearts of the world when he ran out of his side ward to meet the Queen.

Pupils return to school ready to face the future.

Their brave headmaster tells the media that evil has gone and once again his school is a place of learning.

Demolition of the gym where pupils were massacred...

The Angels Sang

The angels sang Amazing Grace,
The Lord came down and touched all your faces,
He whispered soft and low –
"Come with me – its time to go"
The gates of Heaven opened wide,
The angels lined up side by side,
For special guests were on their way,
The morning God brought you all home to stay.
Little angels robed in white,
Give Dunblane primary a kiss tonight.

Dear Dunblane primary one parents
If they had spoken before they died these are the
words that they would have sighed,
"Goodbye my family, my time has passed,
My love for you will always last,
Grieve not for me, but courage take,
And love one another for my sake.
As time goes by and you grow older,
My hands will rest upon your shoulder,
Don't be sad or weep for me."

Dear grandparents relatives & friends
I have only slipped into the other room,
I am I, and you are you,
Whatever we were to each other
that we still are,
Call me by my old familiar name,
Speak to me in the easy way,
Which we always used,
Put no difference in your tone
Wear no forced air of solemnity or sorrow,
Laugh as we always laughed at the
little jokes we enjoyed together,
Pray, smile and think of me,
Pray for them all.

Mrs Mary Gilroy
Co. Leitrim, Ireland

OUR SORROW

We cannot feel the horror
  Nor can we feel the pain
We can only express our sorrow
  To the people of Dunblane.
Sixteen young lives taken from them
  In ten minutes that caused such pain.
Sweet and gentle children
  Whom in this world we will not see again.
Their lives had only started
  Their day had just begun
But they were taken from us
  Very quickly one by one
Let's not forget their teacher
  Who also gave her life
She died helping these children
  A loving mother and a wife
What about the mothers and the fathers
  And the relations left behind
We must all try to help them
  And be understanding, gentle, kind
Let us pray for the injured
  Suffering and still in pain
And hope that one day very soon
  They will be well again
And when our days are over
  And this world we must depart
I know in Heaven we will find these children
  That we keep within our heart.

Susan E. Conley
Morpeth, Northumberland

Dont Let Us Forget

Their smiling upturned faces,
  Their twinkling innocent eyes,
The unconditional love they give,
  Their laughter and their cries.

We take it all for granted,
  With every passing day,
Never for a minute, thinking,
  It could all be taken away.

When you kiss your child goodnight,
  And they hug you and whisper your name,
Take time to stop and remember,
  The innocent children of Dunblane.

Karen Leitch
Argyll

A Prayer

Dear Lord, look after the
  Wee ones, of Dunblane
And keep them safe.
  In Heaven until their
Loved ones can join them.
  Take care too of their
teacher Gwynne – a brave
  brave woman. Amen.

Gordon, 14
Hastings, Sussex

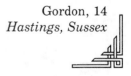

I am sitting with tears running
down my face, Every time I
read a letter or story about the
Dunblane children and their teacher.
If it is hurting me, what on earth
is it doing to the parents and relatives?
I can't imagine.

Stop buying toy guns for your children
it can only promote aggressiveness. In
time there will be no demand for them.
Teach your children to be gentle and
caring. They will grow into responsible
adults, not monsters like that beast who
shot down innocent people.

My son never had war toys. He now has
no interest in them whatsoever.

GUNS KILL!

Gun licensing rules should be stricter.
Guns should only be used in highly
authorised circles, why allow them to be
taken home? What could anyone possibly do
with a gun when its at home?

If guns were harder to acquire there would
be less murders, less rapes, less suicides,
less armed robberies. What a nicer place
our planet would be.

My heart goes out to Dunblane.
GOD BLESS YOU ALL.

D. PARKER.

DEAR MUMS OF DUNBLANE

Those dear little angels will sleep in Heaven tonight,
  For their parents on earth how long is the night?
An ocean of tears will flow from their eyes,
  While their little babes are asleep in the skies.

So unfair it all seems, how cruel life can be,
  That a man so unkind was allowed to roam free,
Tonight so many hearts left shattered in ruin,
  All because of this evil man's doing.

And as the stars shine brightly tonight in the sky,
  May the Lord God check these children don't cry,
Their mummies and daddies will send all their love,
  As their babes sleep up in Heaven above.

Nancy Walls
Poole, Dorset

There is an understandable temptation to turn our schools into fortresses – but I believe that it would be a mistake. Our children must be free to learn and grow in as natural an environment as possible. In the meantime society must be more vigilant to deal with the likes of Tom Hamilton.

Archie Simpson,
Manchester

Forget the arts and sports, let the Lottery money be sent to the people of Dunblane and the local hospitals who coped admirably with such a terrible tragedy.

F. Baker
Hounslow, Middx

I am a mum of two and a grandma of two and my heart is heavy with grief and love. We musn't blame God for this awful thing but ask him to come into our hearts to help ease the pain.

Margaret
Habrough, Humberside

For The Angels Of Dunblane

Who can explain the reason why,
　　Sixteen little children had to die,
A crazy madman with no thought for life,
　　Let loose in a world where killing is rife.

Who knows of the thoughts that ran through his brain,
　　What was the cause? What caused the strain?
Mothers and fathers bowed down with sorrow,
　　He had no thoughts of their empty tomorrows.

Sixteen little ones no longer here,
　　How many more must now live in fear?
When will the world put a stop to the pain?
　　While men can use guns it could happen again.

I pray the world leaders will listen and learn,
　　And make men aware of their growing concern,
That the sorrow and grieving will eventually cease,
　　So our children can grow and enjoy life in peace.

Audrey Robins
Brentford, Middlesex

We are two inmates in prison who would like, on behalf of ourselves, the officers and the several hundred inmates, to express our deepest sympathy to the parents and families of Dunblane.
A fund has been set up by the inmates and although we realised regretably this won't bring the children back we sincerely hope it helps through times of grief. Deepest, deepest sympathy. We are all truly very sorry and you ARE in our prayers. NEVER will your children be forgotten.
Words cannot say how we feel today,
When the Lord came down and took you away,
Our hearts are broken,
with words left unspoken,
memories of you will always live on.
God will guide you now that you're gone.

Steven Whitney and Matthew Childs
H.M. Prison, Hull

A SILENT PRAYER

Let us say a silent prayer for the children of Dunblane,
   For their parents, family and classmates,
Who whisper all their names,
   For their fragile, precious lives cut tragically so short,
Let us keep Dunblane forever in our thoughts.

As you look up at the sky at night, you'll see,
   Sixteen very special stars twinkling so bright.

Let us say a silent prayer for the children of Dunblane,
   And their very special teacher calling them all by name,
All dancing with the angels, giggling with delight,
   Climbing rainbows, catching clouds, flying snowy kites.

We will never ever forget the children of Dunblane,
   In our memories glowing a steady, silent flame.

At night as we switch out our lights,
   Our thoughts and prayers are with them,
Goodnight little darlings - sleep tight.

Mrs Pat Taylor
Aldershot

I was shocked to find out that Tom Hamilton was a Scout leader. I too run a Scout troup and could never hurt any child.

The reason most of us do the job is because we care about children and want to see them grow into healthy, happy, caring adults. Please pass on my condolences to the families of the Dunblane children.

W. D. Hayes
Middx

No More Fears

Oh God why did they die? They were babes why God why?
  School gates they will never walk through no more
But through the gates of Heaven, God at the door.
  No watching them grow up through the years.
Gone is the laughter, house full of tears
  It will never be the same
All you have left is the memories and pain
  But for the sake of others still on this earth
Like brothers and sisters, and new births
  You must carry on with a brave face
Cry now and then in a quiet place
  Let all your grieving come pouring out
Some days you will want to scream and shout
  But there's always that special place in your heart
For all those little angels their journey starts
  They have gone to a place,
Where there are no days or years
  No more guns, no more fears
Think of them as living
  In the hearts of those they touched
Nothing loved is ever lost
  Because they were loved so much
God bless them all.

Maureen Ellen Williams
Plaistow

I write to give my deepest, deepest sympathy to the parents who have lost their children in the worst way imaginable.
These poor children had their lives ahead of them but that was taken away in a few nightmarish minutes. I, like millions of others, wish time could be turned back so we could somehow save those innocent lives.

Lorraine Jeffery
Caterham, Surrey

No more laughter just lots of tears
Unable to watch the children grow up through the years

Despair and sorrow the pain impossible to bear

Sixteen sweet angels now in God's care

The childrens room's left just as they are
Every parent, family, friend will carry the scar,
The evil that came we will never forgive
Because those sixteen sweet angels should have had long lives to live.

Miss M Bell
Stoke-on-Trent

I was travelling in the United States and Canada when the news broke, dominating television and radio broadcasts day after day. When people heard my Scottish accent they took time to talk and offer support. The whole of North America was behind us – the good to come out of this evil was that it united the world.

Derek Gray,
Aberdeen

NEVER AGAIN

We wonder what this world's come to,
    Can anyone ease the pain?
Those babies are now gone forever,
    Innocent victims of Dunblane.

Why did it have to happen?
    Their teacher has gone with them too,
Sixteen little angels were taken,
    There was nothing anyone could do.

She's gone to take good care of them,
    Just like she did, when she was here,
She'll wrap her arms around them all,
    And free them all from their fear.

It's the mums and dads that are left behind,
    They are left to carry the pain,
Every man, woman and child is left numb,
    It must never happen again.

Christine Clare
Warrington

As the managers of the Rum Pot Bar in Tenerife I would like to express our sorrow and devastation felt by the many, many customers, ourselves and staff.
Sitting here in sunshine but no sunshine in our hearts or eyes, the tragedy of Dunblane came to Tenerife. Grown men with a pint in their hands who cannot read any more, women who had to ring home to speak to children.....in this bar we made a collection which has now been taken via a lovely Scottish holidaymaker to be banked for the Dunblane Fund, not a vast sum of money but a vast amount of thought from many upset people.
God give Dunblane the strength to face the future so that the sunshine that is here will shine once more in the hearts of the bereaved.
We in Tenerife care,
Sincerely,

Rosemary and Nigel Smith, Staff and Customers
The Rum Pot, Las Algas San Eugenio
Playa de las Americas, Tenerife

DEVASTATION OF DUNBLANE

No loving arms to hold them,
　No loving kisses to share,
The grief, the horror and the pain,
　Is all too much to bear,
Our hearts go out towards you,
　Our love to you we will share.

Everyone feels your sorrow,
　This cruel world is so unfair,
No mother's arms around them,
　Their lonely hearts they ache,
There is no sense or meaning,
　It is so hard to take.

Your dear little children,
　they faced a terrifying task,
But why our little children,
　we blame ourselves and ask,
Innocent little kiddies,
　went of to school that day.

But, oh, dear God what a terrible price
　they all did have to pay.
Out of the blue came a madman,
　an evil gutless lout.
He fired the bullets of his gun
　and wiped the children out.

The little ones were terrified,
　they stood around so numb
The horror and the agony
　everyone struck dumb.
Some were fatally injured
　others scarred for life
They also lost a teacher
　who was a mother and a wife.

We hate that murdering coward
　we spit upon his corpse,
Because what that evil madman did
　will always bring remorse.
This terrible terrible tragedy
　in all our hearts remain
No one in the whole wide world
　will ever express the pain.

Please believe us people of Dunblane
　as deepest sympathy is expressed
There is truth in the saying that God
　only takes the best.
All our hearts and thoughts are with you
　all along the way
No one will ever ever forget the tragedy
　that struck Dunblane that day.

Marcia B. Edwards
Cardiff

I CRIED

I heard the news
    I sat I cried
I felt something die
    deep inside
Why the children
    why take them
Part of the human race
    lost again
Children a joy to behold
    Not to be put
out in the cold
    In adult life
Lets not forget
    all the children
We need to protect
    My deepest thoughts
    are with you all
In years to come
    you will recall
The fondest memories
    of them all
I heard the news
    I sat I cried
Yes something did die
    deep inside.

Andy Hill
Dagenham, Essex

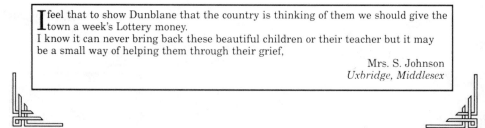

I feel that to show Dunblane that the country is thinking of them we should give the town a week's Lottery money.
I know it can never bring back these beautiful children or their teacher but it may be a small way of helping them through their grief,

Mrs. S. Johnson
Uxbridge, Middlesex

DUNBLANE

We dressed our bairns this morning,
To take them to their school,
We wrapped them all up warmly,
The weather was so cool.

Some of us had grumbled,
Because they were so slow,
Some of us had shouted –
But we were not to know.

That this would be the last time
We'd see their smiling faces,
When we dropped them off it should have been,
One of the safest places.

Forgive us if we doubt you Lord,
We don't know the reason why,
You have taken our children from us,
To live with you in the sky.

You must be short of Angels,
To need our children so,
We didn't know this morning,
That it was their time to go.

We know you only loaned them,
To teach us how to smile,
But could we not have kept them,
For just a little while.

We never will forget them,
They'll be in our hearts forever,
May they be happy there in Heaven.
Until we are together.

Selina Hopkins
London

HEARTS OF GOLD

As I close my eyes I can picture their faces,
　In that school photo, so many spaces,
Those little bairns, all happy and sweet,
　Neat and tidy from head to feet.

Our hearts are with you in your time of need,
　And my tears flow free as the papers I read,
Don't be ashamed and let your tears flow,
　Let your emotions and feelings show.

Gwenne Mayor tried her best to defend them,
　A lovely woman, in one word - a gem.
You'll have to be strong for the ones left behind,
　Just be gentle, understanding - and ever so kind.

Times will be hard and you'll really feel down,
　But put a brave face on, try not to frown,
Your children are safe now, free from all pain,
　The time will come when you'll meet up again.

Think of the good times, not the bad,
　Look back on the happy and not on the sad,
Remember your children, cheerful and bright,
　And at the end of the tunnel, there is light.

Your bairns are in Heaven, in peace, at rest,
　The place they're at is reserved for the best,
God be with you each night, every day,
　And in my heart for you all I'll pray.

Please don't lose faith in the whole Human Race,
　Look back on your bairns with a smile on your face,
Remember them playing, having fun with their mates,
　And they're safe in the Arms of the One who waits.

Lynn Darling
Gateshead

ANGELS ASLEEP

When I first heard the news,
   I was so shocked that I cried,
Why has this happened?
   All those infants had died,
It saddens me greatly,
   That the last thing they saw,
Was their teacher and friends,
   Lying dead on the floor,
Children are so priceless,
   And should be showered with love.
They are gifts out of Heaven,
   And dreams from above,
The parents and loved ones
   Of these angels asleep,
Should cry and cry,
   If it helps them to keep
The memories, all good ones,
   Of their babies at play,
That will help them to get through
   Just one more day.

I cannot begin to imagine
   Just how empty they feel,
But the love and the sympathy
   We all send are so real.

Theresa Christodoulou
Chingford, London

If we parents and grandparents who live many miles away from Dunblane cannot sleep at night because of the horror, how can we expect the parents of these beautiful dead and injured children to sleep?

One cannot imagine the bottomless pit of grief that they must now struggle to escape from.

Words are inadequate but I know the sympathy and prayers of the nation are with them all.

J. Norfolk
Knottingley, W. Yorks

Little Angels Of Dunblane

Such wee small bairns,
    Cheeky, yet sweet,
Hopping and skipping,
    'Long every street.

Some were solemn,
    Some they smiled,
Others stood and mused a 'while.

All were happy,
    Eager and gay,
Off to school,
    Later to play.

No more their happy smiling faces,
    Shall we ever see:
Sitting in their classrooms,
    In their very special places!

Each one will be sadly missed,
    Every morning not there to be kissed,
Life has changed in one short week
    Tears must flow,
Compassion we seek.

Freda J. Ringrose
Spalding, Lincs

God Bless

For all the people of Dunblane,
    All of us share in your pain,
A tragedy beyond belief,
    So much sadness, so much grief,
As the innocent ones are laid to rest,
    Goodnight sweet angels and God bless.

J. Pritchard
Gwynedd

FAR AND NEAR

I feel so far away
  And yet I feel so near
For all those poor children
  Who died with no time for a tear

My heart goes out to all of Dunblane.
  I can hear those poor people saying:
"God, that's my wean".

I never knew Britain could be so close
  This is when we want friends
When you need them most.

I want to thank everybody
  For showing concern
For thanks be to God
  It could have been our bairn.

Here's to a nation,
  Who can be quite tame,
Let's pray for those people,
  Who come from Dunblane.

James Smith
A Scotsman, living in
S.W. London

I am writing this letter to the citizens and the bereaved parents of Dunblane. I was shocked with fear when I heard the appalling news of your sad loss. As a person from Northern Ireland I was gutted to hear how one man can take so many lives.
Men who commit acts of violence and brutality against innocent lives will be judged by God when the time comes and be condemned to Hell.
I know in my heart this letter will not ease the suffering you are going through, but my prayers are with you.

Hugh and Gwen
Belfast

THE BAIRNS OF DUNBLANE

Why all of them?
  One man can cause such mayhem
Why all of them?
  Bairns at their best
Why all of them?
  Gone before their time, laid to rest
Why all of them?
  Now in heaven blest
Why all of them?
  No longer here to jest
Why all of them?
  No more babies in the nest
Why all of them?
  No more to face their quest
Why all of them?
  Too soon little angels laid to rest
Why all of them?
  Little lives full of zest
Why all of them?
  Parents grief put to the test
Why all of them?
  Too soon in heavenly rest
Why all of them?
  They only take the best
Why all of them? Why?

Doreen Coates
Durham

The people of Dunblane should know that the entire nation is behind them in these, their darkest days. Please accept our love and support as you try to come to terms with your sorrow.

Rachel
Maidstone, Kent

GOD BLESS YOU

The lives of little children,
  So cruelly snatched away,
Will remain in people's minds,
  Forever and a day.

Angels must be needed,
  For Heaven up above,
To be taken, oh so tragically,
  From the ones they love.

Words cannot express,
  The sorrow and the pain,
For all the parents left behind,
  Must learn to live again.

The teacher who gave her life,
  So they did not go alone,
Will look after them in Heaven,
  And guide them safely on.

If only miracles could happen,
  We could help to ease their pain.
Let the world unite in prayer,
  For the people of Dunblane.

So sleep now little angels,
  The stars are shining bright
To guide you on your way,
  God bless you and goodnight.

S. Watts
Sutton, Surrey

GENTLE

The children of Dunblane,
  Awakened from their sleeping
By touch of the hands of our Lord Jesus,
  To take in his keeping.
For they now, have been chosen for angels above
  Into the Kingdom of Heaven, the paradise of love.
As you kneel silent in prayer,
  You will be able to reach them there.
They are the stars that twinkle at night
  They are the sun rays that shine so bright.
They are the gentle rustling in the trees.
  They are the rain drops that fall from the clouds
These are the children of whom we feel proud.
  We send them our blessing, we give them our love
To all Dunblane's children in Heaven above.
  Their teacher also now in God's care
We know you are loved, we know you are there.

Mrs C. Finney
Smallthorne, Stoke-on-Trent

WE WILL REMEMBER THEM

Whenever we hear the name Dunblane,
It will always give us great pain,
Thinking of the little angels who lost their lives,
And giving thanks for the ones who survive,
Remembering their teacher who did her best,
To try and protect them, let her soul rest,
May they all be in Heaven doing their gym,
Around the throne of God,
May their memory never dim.

Pearl Hammond, 73
Cirencester, Glos

NIGHTMARE

Their lives had only just begun
  yet God called them to his side,
Wrapped them in his arms,
  Embraced them with love and pride.
They were called away to the
  Lord's playground in the sky,
All so young and innocent,
  we're left wondering why.
The nation grieves with you
  and feels the pain you do.
May God be with you all,
  and memories help you through.
I wish there were words to
  console the pain you feel,
To ease you through the nightmare,
  which is so horribly real.
To lose a child to evil
  must be so very hard to bear
Try to take comfort in knowing,
  there is someone always there.
May your courage never fail
  in your hour of need.
  May you somehow come to terms
  with this evil deed.
Many lives were destroyed
  by this senseless tragedy,
But through your treasured memories
  they'll live eternally.
Not an eye that has not cried,
  a heart that's not felt pain
Not a person who'll ever forget
  the angels of Dunblane.

Tracy Anderson
Edinburgh

♥ FOREVER FRIENDS ♥

Dear Reader, here is my poem by
<u>Kathryn Hardy</u>, 12

Dunblane children

May we pray for the children who died,
The tragedy, the horror, the whole nation
has cried.
May we think for the parents who are
suffering,
Because they have lost their joy and
loving.
Angels is what they are,
Sweet as sugar plum in a jar.
The parent's ask god why?
Why, did my baby have to die.
They could of grown up to be a
real someone,
A doctor, a poet, a person who's fun.
Instead they are with the lord above,
Who will guide them, look after them and
give them love
Hamilton must of been insane,
To murder the innocent children of
Dunblane

On the 17th march at 9.30am,
we' had one minute silence to
rember them.
I'm sure the country will never
forget the day,
when the gun man took the childrens
lives away.
May the children peacefully rest,
As they were the very best.

I went to church on sunday
and I prayed for the children
and the teacher.
Please publish my poem, because
I think people in Dunblane will
feel the same way too.
        Thankyou so much

                    . x .

NEVER EVER WILL YOU BE APART

The loss of the innocent that committed no crime,
    Will always be remembered time after time,
As the 13th of March, was a sad day for Britain,
    You'll always be in our thoughts, this is for certain,
The pain you are enduring, is shared by everyone,
    Not just for one Country, But for the world as one,
The children, the teacher and the families too,
    Our hearts and sympathy goes out to all of you.

I write this poem for the massacred of Dunblane,
    From a heart felt mother, I share your sorrow and pain,
I know nothing, or what people might say, can ever bring them back,
    At least the memories, stay forever and never slack,
For this I believe they'll always be close to your hearts,
    And never ever will you be apart.

Kim Williamson
Winchester

EVIL MAN

All they wanted to do was play,
    But their innocent lives were taken away,
So many ask the question why?
    He was the only one who deserved to die.
An evil man holding a gun,
    What made him take them one by one?
All we have left is heartache and pain,
    Such horror must never happen again.

N. King
Kingston, Surrey

FOR THE LITTLE FLOWERS OF DUNBLANE

I said a prayer for you today
  And know God must have heard,
I found the answer in my heart
  Although He spoke no word.

I didn't ask for wealth nor fame,
  I knew you wouldn't mind,
I asked He send you treasures
  Of a far more greater kind.

I asked that He be with you all
  At the start of every day
To grant you health and happiness
  With friends to share your way.

I asked He give you blessings
  In all things great and small,
But it was for His loving care,
  I prayed the most of all.

The Leaman Family
Brixham, Devon

I sat with my two children aged five and seven having breakfast as I read the full horror of events at Dunblane.

The time was 8.15am. We should shortly be leaving the house for the short trip to school.

Somehow it did not matter that teeth were not brushed, hair not yet combed, school bags and lunch boxes not yet packed.

It did not matter that their bedrooms were littered with clothes and toys.

All that mattered was that Amanda and James were there.

Tears welled in my eyes. "What's the matter, Mum?" asked my son. How on earth do you explain to children about to leave for school what had happened?

My heart goes out to the parents, prayers go out to the injured children.

My love goes out to all those affected by this tragedy.

Mrs Janet Kilgour
Cheylesmore, Coventry

ETERNAL LIFE

In a baby castle,
   Just beyond my eye.
My baby plays with angel toys,
   That money cannot buy.

Who am I to wish him back,
   Into this world of strife.
No, play on my baby,
   You have eternal life.

At night when all is silent,
   And sleep forsakes my eyes.
I'll hear his tiny footsteps,
   Come running to my side.

His little hands caress me,
   So tenderly and sweet.
I'll breathe a prayer and close my eyes,
   And embrace him in my sleep.

No I have a treasure,
   That I rate above all other.
I have known true glory,
   I am still his mother.

Mrs B Kensett
Ashford, Middlesex

As a mother and grandmother – one grandchild a five year old – I felt I had to pen how I felt at this terrible atrocity.
Please print this in your wonderful paper to let those tragic families know that we send them our love and prayers.

Mrs E. Hoare
Havant, Hants

INNOCENCE DESTROYED

Today the world mourns for the bairns of Dunblane,
  A tragedy beyond words to explain,
No words can express how these parents must feel,
  The wounds and the scars that may never heal.

The world sheds a tear for every child,
  Each of them ever so meek and mild,
All of us saddened, shocked and annoyed,
  At innocent lives simply destroyed.

If this is a sign of society today,
  The life of a child is a sick price to pay,
Why did he do it, what did he gain,
  By slaughtering the innocent bairns of Dunblane.

Mrs J.M. Mathison
Rotheram, Yorkshire

LOVED ONES LOST

Angels of innocence,
Just taken away,
From the parents they loved,
And the school where they played.

The world is in mourning,
No word can express
The strength that you need,
With such emptiness.

To see loved ones lost,
It leaves us in pain,
God bless all you darlings,
Who died at Dunblane.

R. Turner
Milton Keynes

No Easy Answer

Ours is not to question,
　Or ask the reasons why,
We will never find the answers,
　No matter how we try.

Each relative remembers,
　Each father and each mother,
The "angels" will live on,
　In each sister and each brother.

Once all the tears subside,
　And all the hate departs,
Their memories will never die,
　Locked safe within your hearts.

Dunblane with all its sadness,
　Will rise and stand again,
United as one people,
　Will find strength amid your pain.

Such inner depth emotions,
　You share with one another,
God stands among you all,
　To help each one recover.

Our thoughts and love are here for you,
　Through all your tears you've cried,
The world awaits, with open arms,
　Standing helpers at your side.

Understanding for each other,
　Will bind you close together,
Your unity will help you through,
　Together, all forever.

Your shared emotions through your lives,
  Will help to ease your pain,
The strength and love, which you have lost,
  Dunblane will find again.

And in the future years to come,
  Together you will stand,
Dunblane will be a stronger place,
  United hand in hand.

Wendy

WEDNESDAY THE 13TH

The Devil came to school today,
  He came to watch the children play,
He chose Dunblane he knew it well,
  He listened for the morning bell,
Those happy children said goodbye,
  To mum and dad you heard their cry.

The Devil came to school today,
  He didn't watch the children play,
He killed them took their innocence,
  For what he did it made no sense,
That Wednesday morning in Dunblane,
  The day your darling babes were slain.

No card for you on Mother's Day,
  No cup of tea on a breakfast tray,
No hugs, no kisses, no one to play,
  Because the Devil came to school that day.

Mrs B. Parkinson
Lowestoft

INNOCENTS

You walked this earth so briefly,
Had your whole lives still ahead,
Your deaths which came so suddenly,
Have left so many words
Still unsaid.

You have all touched our hearts and souls this day,
Your short lives taken with such hateful spite,
And together a nation mourns your loss,
Through the pain of disbelief and grief,
We all unite.

Your families grieve, their pain so deep,
We watch helplessly with despair,
We can only hope our heartfelt thoughts and love,
Will reach out for them to know
We care.

Such senseless acts of violence,
Leave devastation all around,
No questions or answers that can ease the pain,
Shall ever in this life
Be found.

But in memory of each and every precious life,
That was lost upon that day,
Except the beast who took them,
Shall be in all our hearts,
When we pray.

On Mother's Day this Sunday,
My heart will break for those who cry,
Because I can only begin to imagine,
Their tragic loss as they ask themselves,
WHY, "IN THE NAME OF GOD," TELL ME WHY?

K. Paterson
Glenrothes

A Child Is Born

When a child is born they only know how to give,
  Most important of all, they give you a reason to live.

They give you that first little smile, and first steps to walk,
  That big toothless grin, as they struggle to talk.

They give so much in those first few years,
  Laughter, pride and a few little tears.

So why? little children so trusting, innocent and bright,
  Were their lives brutally taken,
Just as if someone turned out the light,
  One man's moment of rage and madness.
Shocked the world and filled it with sadness,
  Our hearts go out to everyone in Dunblane.
We can only stand in the shadows, but we all share your pain.

Mrs Maureen Carson
Southampton

From A Father Who Cares

Children dear children life full of glee,
  A future ahead is what we foresee,
My child I bounced upon my knee,
  A blessing that brought joy to me.

You were my future my dear child,
  Now you are gone we are lost and blind,
You are with the lord safe and sound,
  Beside your friends so small and kind.

Till we meet in Heaven again – Anon
Bathgate

GOD'S CREATION

The anguish, the heartache,
  the tears of a nation.
Children, children,
  God's creation.

No words can express the way we feel.
  Something so dreadful it can't be real.
The innocent victims,
  so sweet, so young.
Somebody's daughter, somebody's son.
  We pray that the parents' pain will ease.

Tarnya Lammin
Ilford, Essex

PRECIOUS MEMORIES

What can I write, what can I say?
  To help ease your pain today.
I feel so shocked and sick and angry
  At the slaughter of your kin.
No one has any answer
  Why this monster did this sin
May love and hugs and kisses envelop everyone.
  May precious memories linger
And strength be never gone.
  All my love.

Isable Panting
Consett, Durham

FIEND FROM HELL

16 little angels,
   Went to school one day,
Little did we know they would
   Never, see another day.
A fiend came out of hell,
   And took their lives away.

The horror of the massacre
   Shocked everyone world wide,
Tears for the anguished parents,
   We shed, and cannot hide.

To every suffering relative
   Our prayers go out to you,
That the sky will turn
   Before too long, from
Deepest grey to blue.

René Lucioni
Lancing, West Sussex

My Charlotte, aged 6, was off school ill the day the tragic news of Dunblane came on the television.
I watched in disbelief and Charlotte asked me why I was crying. I didn't want to alarm her and said some children had been injured in school. She waited a minute and said - but why are you crying since you didn't know them? No, I don't, but I looked at her and felt the pain and still do.
When things like this happen it brings reality back. Life and love are the most precious things in this world and we all at times forget it.
When I took Charlotte back to school I gave her a longer hug and a kiss. I couldn't just lie in bed any more and read articles about this. I had to do something.
Charlotte said, 'Let's do a carboot sale on Sunday and send some money to the Dunblane Appeal.'
Her idea seems so small but if we all pull together something good may come to the children left and all the pupils of Dunblane school.
We will never forget and we as an ordinary family are sending our love and support to all the families, teachers and children of Dunblane.

Mary Seaton
Bournemouth, Dorset

THE INNOCENT ONES

The lives in Dunblane shall never be the same again,
 For we'll remember on the the 13th day
The lives of the babies you took away.
 We ask you Jesus up above why take the people whom we love?
Our lives have gone so far away, no more games shall we play.
 We see no light, no way out. Who-O-why, we all do shout!

Deep inside we feel the pain stabbing us again and again.
 Their tiny faces we'll never see, gone now eternally.
The pain we'll feel, the tears we'll shed,
 no goodnight kisses or tucking you up in bed.
So now dear Jesus it's on you we rely
 to take care of our babies in the sky.
Give them cuddles, kisses and love,
 till we meet again up above.
Until that day we all must try,
 to stick together and help those who cry.

It's time to say good-bye for now, our lives must go on,
 but the question is how? Now that you're gone.

Jill Holt
Burnley Lancs

The Government must reform the laws on possession of handguns following the tragic events in Dunblane.
Why should anyone be allowed to have these weapons in their home?

J. Gibson
Carluke, Lanarkshire

I was at Central Station in Glasgow when the 9.30am minute's silence was observed. The previous day I'd been to see Hearts play Hibs at Tynecastle when there was also a minute's silence. The absolute dignity of everyone on both occasions moved me to tears. Thank God that the vast majority of people are good and decent.

Tom Murray
Edinburgh

FLEETINGLY KNOWN

Could you please pass these words to the parents of Dunblane. We lost a grandson through cot death at just 16 weeks and I know how devastated all our family were. We have a very good child bereavement trust in our area and each year they hold a service for all our lost babies and children. This hymn, Fleetingly Known, was written especially for this occasion and will, I think, hold some meaning to the families of Dunblane who have lost a child.

Fleetingly know, yet ever remembered
   These are our children now and always
These whom we see not we will forget not,
   Morning and evening all of our days.

Lives that touched our lives, tenderly, briefly,
   Now in the one light Living always:
Names in our hearts now, safe from all harm now,
   We will remember all of our days.

As we recall them, silently name them,
   Open our hearts, Lord, now and always
Grant to us, grieving, love for the living
   Strength for each other, all of our days.

Safe in your peace, Lord, Hold these our children
   Grace, light and laughter grant them each day
Cherish and hold them till we may know them
   When to your glory we find our way.

Mrs M. Tillman
High Wycombe, Bucks

LONDON

The Editor
The Sun Newspaper.

19-3-96

Dear Sir,

Re: Enclosed drawing

This thought kept going round in my
head, So I put it down on paper.
I am not much good at drawing,
but I needed to express my feelings.
I hope you will print this in your
paper as my tribute to Dunblane.
It was my 38th Birthday on the 13th
of March, So I will never forget the
babies and their teacher.

Faithfully

Susan Campbell.

EVIL REACHED OUT
AND BROKE THE HEART
OF DUNBLANE

VICTORIA
EMMA
CHARLOTTE
MELISSA
DAVID
KEVIN
BRETT
ABIGAIL
ROSS
MHAIRI
JOHN
MEGAN
EMILY
SOPHIE
JOANNA
HANNAH
GWENNE
MAJOR

AND THE WORLD STRETCHED
OUT IT's ARMS TO
COMFORT AND EASE
THE PAIN

Susan Campbell

117

THE LITTLE CHILDREN

School had just started, For primary one,
  Young hearts beating, ready for fun,
Then an evil man entered, a man with a gun,
  Now, no more laughter, no more sound,
The ominous silence is now all around.

  May God's love enfold them, their teacher too,
We'll pray each day, for each of you.
  God has a garden where you can play,
With Mrs Mayor watching you all each day.

  We feel so helpless, you were taken so young,
One foot on life's ladder, one small step on the rung.
  ARE YOU LISTENING GOD?

They are at your door, please open it wide,
  They're yours ever more, no one can harm them.
In the Lord's arms they sleep,
  While we here on earth, like rivers we weep.
GOD BLESS THE LITTLE CHILDREN.

A Grandmother

The doctors, nurses and all the emergency services deserve the highest praise for their handling of events in the tragic aftermath of Dunblane.
Our sympathies and support goes to all the families. Together may they find strength for the future.

Ellen Davies
Bearsden, Glasgow

Brave teacher Gwenne Mayor deserves the highest honour for her unselfish and brave act, trying to shield her pupils.

J. Bell
Davyhulme, Gtr Manchester

FLOW OF TEARS

The flow of tears grows in Dunblane,
　As families show their hurt and pain,
But even though they all have gone,
　We know their hearts and souls live on.

They wouldn't want to see you cry,
　They'd want to see you push and try,
To be as brave as they had been,
　Before the painful tragic scene.

You have the world's respect and love,
　For all those children up above,
Times have changed and they have gone.

Sherry Counter (13)
Feltham, Middlesex

WHY

Where is the answer when we ask why,
　Those that suffer can only sit and cry,
Words won't ease them, money won't compensate,
　It's hard to forgive, it's hard not to hate,
Time they say will heal as the days go by,
　Will we ever find the answer when we ask,
　　　　　　"WHY"
Can anyone provide the answer?

Joyce Alexander
Langar, Notts

THE ANGELS OF DUNBLANE

Fresh young tender flowers in bud
Yet to bloom into adulthood.
Cherished and protected so we thought,
Never doubting never fraught.

Born into a loving family, a treasure and a joy,
So very, very special, each little girl and boy,
How cruel the blow on that dark evil day,
When a madman came and took them all away.

Oh dear God, please tell my why,
these innocent children had to die?

G Elsmore
Melton Mowbray

SO MUCH PAIN

There is a place called Dunblane
    Where all the people are in so much pain,
There are floods of tears and broken hearts
    There lives have been torn apart.

These people had such bonny babes,
    They went to school to laugh and play,
Then one day while in the gym
    A horrid man just walked in.

Now they're angels up above
    So sadly missed and loved so much,
May they now rest in peace
    And guide you through all your grief.

Heidi Collings
Bow, East London

SLEEP IN PEACE

Sleep in perfect peace dear babies
   In Jesus' arms you lay
While mums and dads wipe their tears
   As silently they pray.

The whole world feels their sorrow
   So many words were left unsaid
We know their heartfelt anguish
   When they see your empty bed.

But God will send his comfort,
   Who gave his only son
And said "Suffer Little Children"
   Unto me you will all come.

Dee Bull
Worthing, West Sussex

As a nursery assistant, I can only try to understand how Dunblane as a city and the bereaved families feel.
I don't know what I would do if anything ever happened to our nursery children. So God only knows how the parents of Dunblane must be feeling.
When I watched the service at Dunblane Cathedral all I could do was cry helplessly for you all. Rest in peace, little children.

Julie Cooke
Bourneville, Birmingham

I have a son who is due to go to school in September. My friend has a son who attends nursery school and he saw the news and didn't want to go. He was going to do PE and didn't want to get shot.
I just want the people of Dunblane to know that we will care and are so sorry for what has happened.

R. Humphrey-Smith
Epson, Surrey

16 LITTLE ANGELS

Dunblane I'd never heard of,
  Its never crossed my mind,
Today I know I'd get there,
  Its so easy to find.

I'd follow the river of tears,
  I'd walk the path of pain,
To help to stop the suffering
  That must never happen again.

Sixteen little angels,
  Taken by the Devil himself,
But God will step in and gently begin
  To lift them to himself.

This sorrow that's felt inside us,
  It's not the pain we bear,
Its for the mums and dads of the kids,
  The kids no longer there.

A caring Dad.

I get choked every time I read the paper or see the news about those children and their teacher. My heart goes out to all their families.
We are holding a raffle in the shop where I work and all the money will be sent to the Dunblane fund.

June McGovern
Taunton, Somerset

May I suggest a new school hall be built and the one where this terrible tragedy happened be made into a chapel of remembrance to honour those tots and their teacher who died and those who were injured.
If I am ever fortunate to go to Dunblane I would go to the chapel and in humility bow my head and pray.
I will think of this tragedy with tears in my eyes for the rest of my life. My prayers go to the families.

Mrs. E. Antcliff
Derby

DEAR FRIENDS

How can we hope to ease your pain
  We envelop your hearts, but I feel in vain
The feelings you feel must be so intense
  Your babies gone forever, it makes no sense.

There are no words for us to say
  There is no prayer that we can pray
We'll never know the reasons why
  This terrible loss just makes us cry.

If there's any comfort to be had,
  Please know that the nice people feel sad,
We want you to know that we feel your grief
  And that our memories will not be brief.

Your children are in Heaven now,
  One day soon, you'll see them somehow,
Their innocence will come shining through
  On a sunbeam one day, right to you.

And while you are waiting for that day,
  Please know that our love's not far away,
Try to bear the pain and sorrow,
  And know that another day will be tomorrow.

Jan
East Sussex

I'm writing to you in shock and horror at these terrible deaths. As the grandmother of a six-year-old boy, it makes me wonder whether our children are safe anywhere. I want to send my heartfelt sympathy to the families of those that died.

Mrs C. May
Lewisham, South East London

To The Families Of Dunblane

We all give a piece of our heart
  We all send you all our tears
No one can replace these lives cut down in years.
  But everyone thinks of you, I always will,
Never forget those children whose beauty is now still.

The world goes on we know
  And the sun will always shine
But the families of these children
  Won't heed these for all time.

They will never forget one minute of the day
  Those lovely bright-faced children as they go on their way
The world will always remember
  And the mothers will always pray.

> From a mother of seven children
> and 18 grandchildren

Why?

Why the pain and torment?
  Why the sorrow deep?
Why unending heartbreak?
  Heads low, hands clasped, we weep.

Flowers and love surround them,
  Strong arms hold them near,
His love is now around them,
  The ones we hold so dear.

Soft petalled dreams bring comfort,
  Sweet memory of loving days,
Within our hearts we hold them,
  They are close - not far away.

> Mrs. Ina Paterson
> *Haxby, York*

LOVE EVERLASTING

Time moved so fast when our children were small,
From season to season it flew.
And months turned to years and soon it was time,
For our little ones to go to school.
And time slipped on by and every new day,
The lessons of life were taught there.
And the teachers had hopes that the future would bring,
Success to each child in their care.

But life suddenly stopped on that fateful day,
As the children lay there on the ground.
Each moment seemed endless - awaiting for news -
But the beat of their hearts made no sound!
And each living second seemed endlessly slow,
As each parent faced stark grief and pain.
For their children and teacher needlessly killed,
And those injured that day at Dunblane.

Now time moves so slowly, for God only knows,
Just how long it will take to heal
The hearts of the people so battered and bruised
By the sorrow and pain that they feel.
But Love is everlasting and stronger than death,
Never failing, eternal and true.
Because love is triumphant, in Heaven you'll find
Your children are waiting for you.

Yvonne Lyons
Greenisland, Carrickfergus

All the parents should be consulted to see if a new school should be built for Dunblane and paid out of National Lottery funds. If they wished the present school could be demolished and replaced by a memorial garden.

Jean
Leven

TEARS ACROSS THE LAND

All across this country's land,
  So many tears we've cried,
And no-one alive could feel
  How much pain you hold inside.

So many things to say to you,
  And not one could ease your pain,
But in our prayers and in our hearts
  The hurt you feel remains.

Our thoughts are with everyone
  Who's world was torn apart,
A country united by sadness and grief
  And the breaking of so many hearts.

Mrs. Emma Towell

FLOW OF TEARS

But even though they all have gone,
  The flow of tears grow in Dunblane,
and families show their hurt and pain,
  We know their hearts and souls live on.

They wouldn't want to see you cry,
  They'd want to see you push and try,
To be as brave as they had been,
  Before the painful tragic scene.

You have the world's respect and love,
  For all those children up above,
Times have changed and they have gone,
  But all their hearts and souls live on.

Sherry Counter (13)
Feltham, Middlesex

A Prayer For The Parents

To sixteen little angels who were so deeply loved
   But yet so horrifically lost.
Your lives were so pure and innocent,
   Your hearts so tender and loving.
You had so much to live for,
   And a whole life ahead of you.
Yet someone so cruel and heartless
   Stole it from you.
Your loss and suffering is shared by us all
   But no words on earth can describe how you feel.
Your lives were so young and precious
   And your hopes and dreams are shattered.
But remember this, there is something so precious
   That he just couldn't take away from you.
They were the memories that will live forever in your hearts.
   God bless you all, and may you rest in peace.
Good night my little angels, you shall never be
   Forgotten and your memories shall live forever
In our hearts.

Clare Stridley
Reading

It has taken a week to write this as every time I think about what I am going to say I cry.

I have three daughters aged 17, 14 and 13 and we have our ups and downs like everyone else but when I saw the photo of your babies it could have so easily been one of mine so all I can do is thank God.

I hope that you gather the strength we are all trying to send you to do what you think is best for the rest of your life.

I have grown up without a mother who died when I was 4 years old. If she had been murdered like your babies I don't know if I could have coped with that.

Our thoughts will be with you always.

Lynn and Brian Goldsmith
Briston, Norfolk

FROM ULSTER WITH LOVE

To all the people of Dunblane,
　We know your sorrow, feel your pain,
Years of bloodshed we have known,
　None to compare with your own.

No matter what life throws our way,
　We will always remember that fateful day,
When lives were shattered one by one,
　By the hand that held the gun.

Friends we've lost and family too,
　But now our thoughts are all with you,
The teacher and each little one,
　The families who've been left to mourn.

Mother
Northern Ireland

HEADS HELD HIGH

God looked down from Heaven up high,
His tears flowed down and fell from the sky,
For towards him came a line so long
　of children full of song.
Their halos new, their heads held high,
Their lady angel standing by,
　guiding them along the way,
To hold hands tight and not to stray.
God raised his hands,
His head he bowed,
His thoughts were deep,
but spoken loud
WHY?

Carol Flaherty
Manchester

A Prayer For The Innocent Bairns Of Dunblane

Suffer little children to come unto Thee, for such is the Kingdom of Heaven & Forbid them not. Dear Reverent Lord Jesus today with saddened hearts we pray for the innocent little victims and teacher that were slain so unmercifully in Dunblane. Also for the wounded. Please Holy One come and comfort all the bereaved, and support them all in their hour of sorrow. Hearts that are so full of agonizing pain and bewilderment, may they turn to you for help. We all pray now for the ones that are left behind that have to face the years of suffering and the loss of their beloved children - heartache and grief. Be at their side Lord when they call out to Thee. Comfort and guide them. And let the little ones rest in peace with thee and your angels above - Amen.

Written with grief in my heart as I have lost my Beloved Husband recently and will sorrow with the people of Dunblane. God Bless you all.

Joyce Taylor
London

IF I COULD GIVE

God, why did you have to take them away,
   Why could you not have let them stay
If there was anything that I could give
 'If only you would let them live.

Those parents the pain they must feel
   The grief inside them is all too real,
Not one person will ever understand
   Why you did not lend them a helping hand.

Only time, if ever, may ease the pain,
   For nothing now will ever be the same,
The shock, the horror will always remain
   For those children from Dunblane.

Mgt. Gray
Beds

A special permanent fund to help deprived children, and carrying the name Dunblane, would be a fitting way to remember the innocent victims.

Sun reader
Norwich

The whole country is grieving with you, precious people of Dunblane – why? we cry – we want someone to blame and rail against for the slaughter of these Angels and the untold damage to the ones who witnessed the carnage.
I saw a message on the TV. God take care of these precious ones as this world never can. And this is true of all our children – and us too!
When God put us on this earth, he gave us a gift of free will – to do good or to do evil – if he intervened every time someone made a bad decision – he would be taking away a very precious gift from us and we would resent him.
God did not want a world of Robots but we should have made a world of love and peace and learn from each other.

With many tears and
love to you all
Margaret
Habrough

NEVER AGAIN

Oh little children of Dunblane
  Whose parents' lives will never be the same,
Though Jesus cries – he must be glad,
  To have the sweetest angels, Heaven's ever had.

And though we mourn, and though we weep,
  And we can't eat, and we can't sleep,
We'll always remember each face and name,
  And pray to the Lord – this never happens again.

Nadia Mason
Cheltenham

NOT ALONE

You are not alone today,
Nor will you be tomorrow,
For warmest thoughts
  of those who care,
Are with you in your sorrow,
And may it comfort you to know
  your loved ones are thought of too,
By everyone who shares a loss
  of one so dear to you.

May knowing that so many
  people share your grief with you,
Help you through this time
  of sorrow and bring comfort too.

I'd gladly loose a limb if it meant those babies and
their teacher being alive today.
  From a mother of three boys who can't stop thinking
    about the families of those in Dunblane.
      My heart is with you all

WHY I CRY

I try not to think about it.
   Try and forget this tragedy has happened.
Because everytime I think of it
   I can't help but cry.
I feel my heart has broken.
   But, it's for children I do not know.
Yet, that doesn't stop my grief,
   That doesn't subside my anger
That doesn't dry my tears.
   I cry for the loss and the waste,
I cry for what might have been,
   I cry for the way they died,
I cry due to the madness in this world,
   I simply cry for those lost babies.
It's because I'm human that I cry
   Unlike that evil maniac who took them away.
I wish I could bring them back.
   I wish I could make everything alright.
I wish I could take away the parent's grief.
   But, like a nightmare this has happened.
We will always cry for those babies lost in Dunblane
   Who died due to a moment's madness.
They will never be far from our thoughts
   Even though they were sent to Heaven to become angels.

Miss E. Cole
East London

In the light of the terrible tragedy at Dunblane don't others agree with us that whatever it costs to knock down and rebuild its gymnasium there, every penny should be met by the National Lottery as it covers sport and leisure. We can't think of any other more deserving cause than this one,

J. and L. Holliday
Leeds

(GWENNE)
A GUIDING STAR AND HER 16 LITTLE ANGELS

NO ONE KNOWS WHAT CAUSED
PAIN ON THAT TRAGIC DAY

NOW 17 NEW STARS ARE SHINING
ALONG THE MILKY WAY

ONE GUIDING STAR IS LEADING
THEM, AS SHE DANCES THE
HEAVENLY PLAIN

FOLLOWED BY 16 SMILING LITTLE
ANGELS
THE CHILDREN OF DUNBLANE

Brian and Zena Keresley
Coventry

ALWAYS

Sixteen children dead. Why?
    Because a monster got a high,
Trying to run, trying to hide,
    Their frightened eyes watching,
The guns by his side.
This shouldn't have happened,
    They are all so young,
But now their last song has been sung.
We will never forget the day,
    The day he took those children away,
They will always be here with you,
    Every day, every night,
And in every thought, too.

Emma Coe
Diss, Norfolk

A TEAR

A single lonely Scottish tear,
    Drops from a Scottish eye,
This single tear speaks more than words,
    From the lips of you or I.

It's from a Scottish mother,
    Who's lost her only child,
A simple little baby,
    So small, so meek, so mild.

This single tear will never dry,
    As her heart will never mend,
We pray dear Lord a little peace,
    To this Scottish mother send.

James Smyth
Belfast

STOLEN LIVES

Those poor lives cruelly stolen, they're
  watching everyone all the time,
They're probably happy up with God,
  He'll look after them till the end,
They shouldn't have died, they should
  have lived,
They love you always, and always will.

Thomas Owens
Ebbw Vale, Gwent

THOUGHTS

My thoughts are with you every day
  Since your babies were taken away.
I cannot imagine how you all must feel
  But the sympathy I send is all for real.

Mrs. V. Cullip
Kent Road, Selby

I'm so full of sorrow and pain for the kids and their families that I feel numb when I try to think about the beast who caused all of this.

Everyone, from ordinary people, MPs, the media and the Royal Family has expressed their feelings in the best way they know, but I couldn't believe it when I heard the hospital Reverend tell everyone to find it in themselves to forgive the killer.

It sounded like he believes God forgives this monster... well, I'm sorry, but on this one God stands alone!

Rest in peace little angels.

Brenda O'Hanlon
Lochgelly, Fife

EMPTY CHAIRS

A Poem for the Children

Do you think you can remember
what it was like when you were young
when you sit back and think about
the games you played for fun.
With your sweetest eyes and your loving smiles
you were young innocent and free
but tonight a part is missing
from the child in you and me.

I remember my first day at school
with a fondness and a thought
of what I owe to all the teachers
and everything they taught.
Now I'm grown into a man
it hurts to see the chairs
sitting in them only loneliness
where children once were there.

Anon

SUFFER THE LITTLE CHILDREN

They were little angels here on earth, both loved and adored,
  Suffer the little children to come to me, said the Lord,
They are little angels still, in everybody's eyes,
  Albeit, by God's grace, with Him, in Paradise.

They were so very young, so pure, and wholly innocent,
  Priceless, precious gifts from Heaven, but alas, were only lent
To parents here on Earth, all filled with bursting pride,
  Never to understand the reason or forget the day they died.

They were so full of life, to all who knew and loved them,
  Be not ashamed to weep or those teardrops stem,
They are forever young, wherever they may be,
  Little angels now, please God, with Thee eternally.

Mr P. Blaes
Mablethrope, Lincolnshire

I suppose this must be the ten thousandth letter you have received about the Dunblane disaster. My heart goes out to the families of those beloved children but you have to ask the question: 'Why has this been allowed to happen?"

Shouldn't we have learned our lessons when that great headmaster was killed? And when that little girl was stabbed two years ago?

There has been enough talk to last a lifetime over the past week. What we need now is action.

If it takes a ten-foot wall around our schools and security guards on every entrance then that's what we should do.

I have a two-year-old child and I shudder for her future. Surely no amount of money is too much to protect our children?

S. Knighton
Lincoln

Suffer Little Children

Those beautiful flowers cut down too soon,
Not even had time to grow and bloom.
Parents and Relatives so loving and caring
in their grief we'll be sharing.
We will support them with our thoughts and prayers,
Please let them know that you still care,
Why ! dear lord did-this have to be.
They were but babies blameless and free,
The clouds came over, tears fell like rain,
How can we ever feel the same.
Their brave teacher also lost her life,
Shielding the children while bullets were rife,
God surround these families with your love,
And bless these little ones playing in heaven above

Mrs. E.J. Hoare.
Havant, Hants

I am sure there were many tears shed everywhere over Dunblane and I'm sure we could all help in a small way to remember.
I thought how wonderful it would be if every year on the anniversary of the Dunblane tragedy you could announce a request for all people who would like to take part to plant a handful of flower bulbs at the side of the road wherever they choose so the tragic parents would see the flowers and know how many wonderful people were reaching out to them in their grief and what a lovely show it would make in memory of those children for all of us.

J. A. Coyston
Dunmow, Essex

Newport.
Gwent.

Dear Sir

My idea of a perfect remmembrance for the children of "Dunblane".

Surely there is a small patch in the school grounds ~~of~~ or some where near where mothers and farthers could plant one of the beautiful coloured primulas that are in bloom at present.

These children should not and will not be forgotten this way. Every year as the flowers open their faces it would be as if the children are saying "Hello Mummy".

As it is now the lovely flowers that line the road will soon be cleared all away and swept clean.

Just a mother of a precious bin

Ann Brown.

139

LITTLE ANGELS

On school days they would be together and play.
  Fun and laughter to hear,
young hearts filled with joy and cheer.

Never can words say the loss and grief we feel.
  Taken, these wee bairns have gone,
yet in their loved ones' hearts they live on.
  Candles that burn bright
and together form a greater light.

Close your eyes and you will see sixteen wee bairns,
  Boys and girls, little angels, at play in God's perfect world.

May they live on forever in Heaven.

Anon

I am ten years old and I go to primary school. I have two younger brothers, Ben, aged eight and Jamie, aged six, who is the same age as you.
We should be safe at school not scared. School should be a place to be happy. The man who did this should go to hell and the children in Mrs Mayor's class will go to heaven in peace. How could any man take the lives of innocent children?
Why did he have to shoot young school-children?
I hope you all get better. Everyone is thinking of you. Get well soon, children of Dunblane.

Zoe Manning
Sidcup, Kent

I felt I had to write this letter, what happened in Dunblane has upset me so very much. My heart goes out to those parents and friends of those beautiful children.
I just hope the IRA were watching the news and realise that all the unnecessary blood-shed should stop.
I'm glad Hamilton killed himself because someone else would surely have pulled the trigger. What is the world coming to?

Lee Duffy
Welwyn Garden City, Herts

IN GOD'S CARE

No more laughter just lots of tears
  Unable to watch the children grow up through the years.
Despair and sorrow the pain impossible to bear
  Sixteen sweet angels now in God's care
The children's rooms left just as they are
  Every parent, family, friend will carry the scar
The evil that came we will never forgive
  Because those sixteen sweet angels should have had long
lives to live.

Anon

I felt I had to write this. I am a typical mum with twin boys, who are now five and at full-time school, and a little girl of eight.
Our mornings start with shouting and constant nagging to get them out of bed.
They come down at their own pace – no hurry or worry about the fact they may be late for school. I am the only one who worries about that.
So you rush off to school, you kiss them in the playground and say: "Have a good day."
Sometimes you are glad they are going because they have fought in the car and you long for a bit of peace and quiet.
However, after hearing the news about the poor little children in Scotland – the same ages as my boys – I cried.
No matter what disruptions we have in the mornings, I always know they will be there at 3.15pm when I pick them up.
I look forward to them coming home so we can plan our weekends etc. It is taken for granted.
All I can say is that my children had extra love and cuddles tonight.
Maybe one day they won't be there and that's a lesson to us all.
Don't take life for granted, you never know when it will be taken away from you.
My heart goes out to all those parents in Scotland.

Susan Jackson
Helston, Cornwall

THEY SAY

They say that "things are meant to be".
   That life depends on Fate:
But who could guess
   'Twould be so soon
Or even on that date...
   Sixteen tiny people
Who'd just learnt to read and write,
   Left home that Wednesday morning
And soon were gone from sight.
   Their teacher tried to guard them
Like a shepherdess with her flock.
   What fear was in her mind then?
As Destiny watched the clock.
   Their time on Earth had ended,
They've gone home to whence they came,
   For all the people in Dunblane
Life will never be the same.

The world outside this 'normal' town
   Looked on with heavy hearts.
What could we do to help those left,
   Whose lives are ripped apart,
Those parents who, bewildered, broken,
   Cry out with grief so strong,
Must hate this 'man' who, though quite
   Mad, has done such evil wrong.
And even those most Christian who have
   No cause to doubt the simple love
Of Jesus - God - just "WHY?" they need to shout.

These tinies and Gwenne Mayor
  Are in the best of places.
The light of Heaven is on them
  And shines, warm on their faces.
They feel the touch of healing hands
  To hold them safe with care.
Their spirits soar to heights anew
  Back home - with Jesus there.

For the little ones injured
  And the teachers too
I send out my prayers
  So that you'll be whole too,
That the memories you've witnessed
  May be no longer seen
And your lives will be healthy, long -
  A tribute to the seventeen.

Teresa Bonner
Buntingford, Herts

I have penfriends in Australia, Canada and Hong Kong who have all written to express their shock and deep sadness over what happened and to say how everyone in their communities sends their prayers to Dunblane.

Kevin Mitchell
Liverpool

Dear God, please send hope, love, peace, serenity and courage to Dunblane and its shattered people. Let them know they have the love and caring of all Britain and the entire world behind them.

Michelle Evans
Luton

Every parent with schoolchildren must be worried after Dunblane. There will be much talk of security cameras and security guards in our schools. Perhaps we should build high walls with security gates. OK, they would seem like prisons. But our children would be safe.

Freda Page,
Flackwell Heath, Bucks.

FLY

Fly, fly little wings,
  Fly beyond imaginings,
The softest cloud, the whitest dove,
  Upon the wind of Heaven's love
Past the planets and the stars,
  Leave this lonely world of ours,
Escape the sorrow and the pain
  And fly again.

Fly, fly precious one,
  Your endless journey has begun,
Take your gentle happiness,
  Far too beautiful for this,
Cross over to the other shore,
  There is peace forevermore
But hold this mem'ry bitter sweet
  Until we meet.

Fly, fly, do not fear,
  Don't waste a breath, don't shed a tear,
Your heart is pure, your soul is free,
  Be on your way, don't wait for me
Above the universe you'll climb,
  On beyond the hands of time,
The moon will rise, the sun will set
  But I won't forget.

Fly, fly little wing,
  Fly where only angels sing,
Fly away, the time is right,
  Go now, find the light.

Mrs S. Adams
Sholing, Southampton

DEAR LITTLE CHILDREN

Dear little children
  You shouldn't have died.
I see all your faces
  And openly cry.
Innocent babies
  Slain by man's evil hand,
How can we forgive
  When we don't understand.
Your short lives are over,
  Just finished and done.
You'll never get married
  And have daughters and sons,
Dear mummies and daddies,
  Your grief I do share
But your babies live on
  In God's tender care.
You must try and forget
  That terrible day
When your dear little children
  Were taken away.
I am a mum and a nanny too,
  All night long I have wept for you,
I know the pain will stay in your heart,
  The day you and your babies had to part.
God bless you all in your time of pain,
  One day you will all learn to smile again

Wendy Gibbs
Brighton, Sussex

DUNBLANE'S ANGELS

Now round the world we all cry
   For the children that lost their lives,
So small, so full of life,
   And now they are gone.
Oh! What a waste of life,
   To think that a man,
If I can call him one,
   Could do as he has done.
Our hearts go to the parents
   And playmates left behind
But in our hearts the children
   Will angels always stay,
On holy ground they play.
   We will never forget them
Till the end of our days
   But what we write can't help
The ones that are left behind.
   But it may help to show them
That the world does all care
   For the little angels
That now fly in the air.

Pauline Haggett
Bridport, Dorset

I wish I could have been in that room instead of those poor children. But all I can do is cry and pray for them.
I am a Christian but that does not stop me from feeling hatred for the man who did this. I hope his soul suffers forever and a day,

R.C. Dunstan
St. Leonard-on-Sea, East Sussex

SADNESS

So small, so sweet, so innocent,
　　So young to have life taken away,
In just a few minutes in one day,
　　They went to school where they
Should have been safe and happy.

Instead for so many mums, the day ended very unhappy,
　　In Dunblane there is a lot of sadness and grief,
But all our prayers have been answered with relief.
As the animal that ended so many young and innocent lives,
　　Turned the gun upon himself and died.

Mrs L. Darren
Kirkintilloch, Glasgow

BRAVE

Hush and listen, where is the noise
　　It's so quiet, without these girls and boys.
They were so tiny, life just starting
　　It's a terrible thing, to have such parting.
My heart says, they will have much love
　　arms wrapped around them from the Lord above
Hold them tightly, in every way.
　　They should never have been taken in this way.
To all their families, teachers too
　　My anger is felt along with you.
Grief and sorrow comes from us all.
　　To show we felt for those so small.
Our love and thoughts are much the same.
　　As the **Brave Brave** people of **Dunblane**.

Mrs June Meachem
Litterworth, Leics.

A POEM FOR PRIMARY ONE

My heart weeps,
　My eyes cry,
Why did it happen,
　Why did they die,
Why them so innocent and young,
　Why take their lives,
When they had only just begun.
　Why take their love; so tender and sweet,
Why take away their clapping hands,
　And the pit-ta pat-ta of their tiny feet.
Why take their smiles,
　Why take their joys,
Why take those darling little girls and boys.
　Why take their laughter when they were having fun,
Why take away someone's daughter,
　Why take away someone's son.
Why take their trust,
　Their hopes and dreams,
Why such a tragic loss,
　Senseless it all seems.
And why take their teacher who taught in class,
　Why seventeen precious lives,
Shattered like glass.
　Why...I do not know,
I don't think I ever will,
　But those of Primary One
Are in my prayers still.
　Sweet dreams, little angels,
God bless you all,
　All my love.

R. J. Newland
Weymouth, Dorset

LOVE'S LAST GIFT

You will dance again,
  Sweet little ones of Dunblane,
You will twirl with the sun
  And skip with the rain,
Your smiles have left a permanent ray
  By night in the moonlight,
In sunlight by day.

You will sing again,
  Sweet little ones of Dunblane,
Your sighs will be carried by the midsummer's breeze,
  Your tiny footsteps in the whispering trees,
Your words will be preached in churches and heard
  And your songs will be sung by the humming bird.

You will live again,
  Sweet little ones of Dunblane,
In your mummies and daddies you will always remain
  Within the hearts of millions you will always be
Because love's last gift is memory.

We will see you again,
  Sweet little ones of Dunblane,
When we all finally reach God's heavenly plain,
  There we will live together and free
In the warmth of God's great family.

                                        Rachel Katex

SWEET LITTLE ANGEL

The sky that is up in Heaven
  Must be short of angels and God, He must
Have been all on his own.
  For now Heaven must have sixteen
Little angels
  And God will never be alone.
The joy is that they will always
  Be together,
Playing from cloud to cloud,
  For secrets they will always have
Just being with one another,
  The sky ringing out loud
On this Mother Earth, things will never
  Be the same,
Also for the grief-stricken city of
  Dunblane,
Sweet little children were always playing
  Together
For now they are in God's arms being
  Cuddled forever and ever,
For when they were in this life they all
  Had respect
For every one of these little angels
  The rest of the world must never
Forget.

Jay Cole
Langley, Slough

A Nation Cried

Their lives will never be the same,
    Their dreams were shattered
And replaced with pain.

Seventeen families lost a pot of gold,
    Sixteen of those only five years old.

Murdered by a devil, a demon, a fiend,
    Not caring about the heartache
Or loss it would bring.

Their teacher tried but all in vain
    To save these angels from all pain,
She lost her life in her attempt
    So brave, so loving, she was heaven-sent.

Mrs B Lambert
Hanwell, London

A Prayer

Dear God, please love and protect the innocents of Dunblane
who were so tragically cut down. Give their loved ones the
courage and strength to try and cope with their terrible ordeal.
Give the people of Dunblane hope and inspiration for the future
and the will to carry on. Amen.

Rachel Martin, aged 10
Richmond, Surrey

STOLEN LAUGHTER

Ten little fingers,
  Ten little toes,
How can anyone take away those,
  The joy and the laughter
Turned to sorrow and pain,
  My heart will always remember Dunblane.
A very brave teacher, mother and wife,
  I am sure she would have been the best
If she had continued her life.
  The very hard labour
For girl or boy
  Now very elated, full of joy,
Their tiny faces full of glee,
  Tiny tears, silly me,
How can anyone take away these,
  My heart feels broken
For mums and for dads,
  For brother and sister,
And grandparents too.
  What will this little community now ever do?

> Mrs T A Halliday
> *Nottingham*

Like a whole nation, I am still in a state of shock. I have cried too many times to count.

I want the Mums, Dads, husband and daughters and all the relatives of all the little children and their teacher to know that they are being thought of and prayed for.

We are all so very sorry.

I started to feel anger at the politicians and authorities which allowed this evil man access to guns.

I, like so many others, want to know -
Why? Why? Why?

> Patricia Hill
> *Buckingham*

GUNMEN

A man who was insane went crazy in Dunblane,
   Blasted the innocents,
Now ask who is to blame?

It only needed one madman with a gun
   To walk into the school
And his evil deed was done.

Our country weeps today
   And its shocked people pray
For the parents of the kids
   Slaughtered in this way.

I'm not the only one who's never seen a gun,
   Who wants these deadly weapons?
Who wants to shoot for fun?

It only needs one madman with a gun.

Betty Blacklaw
Swansea

My name is Sarah Williamson and I am 19 years old. I work as an ancillary assistant at St. Mary's R.C. School in Grantham in the reception class with the four to five-year-olds and I love it and enjoy working with children. I've been here for about two and a half years.

It is because I work with children that I am doing a sponsored walk from my house to Woodsthrope and then back which is about 16 miles altogether to raise funds for the Dunblane Fund that you are running.

I hope me raising this money will help their parents, families and also friends to overcome their deaths.

I know the hurt inside will never go away because I lost my cousin who was only 13 about five and a half years ago. I still miss him now and I cannot seem to let him go. I think on my birthday especially that he should be as old as me. I hope by me doing this walk the money will help them in some way.

Sarah Williamson
Grantham, Lincs

Dear The Sun

I felt I had to write this letter, as what happened
on Wednesday 13th March in Scotland upset me very
much. My heart goes out to those Parents and Friends
of all those beautiful children. And I just hope the IRA
are watching the News and then they will realize all
the unnecessary blood shed should stop. If it doesn't
affect their hearts like the rest of the world then
they did not human, But Robots. Also I'm glad the man
killed himself, because Somebody else would of pulled the
trigger.

. What is this world coming too .

Lee Duffy
Mother of 2
Welwyn Garden City, Herts

We Senior Citizens, were
Shocked & Horrified by the
Dunblane Disaster of last
Wednesday.

We have cried so much for
you & having to bear so much
suffering, ai the loss of your
dearly loved & beautiful
children.

We feel so helpless to
express our grief, other than to
light a single candle ai
the one minute's silence.

Also this is for their teacher
& Family.

Our prayers & thoughts will
always be with you, & we
pray God will be with you
always

G. F. and V. L. Blagg
Danlish, Devon

Up And Down

Up and down the country
  We weep
For little children
  Not asleep
Of their own accord -
  But -
Asleep forever
  By an evil hand.
They have been enfolded in arms of love
  By parents and family
Who shall always remember them.

A Grandmother
Oxford

All Alone

The media gone and you're all alone,
  Your babies at rest in their wonderful home,
In God's care till the end of time
  I know you will feel - 'they were only mine!'

You are so brave to have lived through these days,
  Life will go on in a dreadful haze,
Together in Heaven one day you will be
  Then once again your world will be free.

Jane Bladon
Spinney Close near Coventry

SHORT LIVES

In life though short
   They played together,
They died together so
   Let them rest and lay together,
Angels will watch over them
   On their journey to Heaven.

Mrs S Howe
Plymstock, Plymouth

IF ONLY

If only I could see your face.
   If only I could dry your tears,
If only I could kiss your lips,
   If only I could hear your voice.
But now you're gone, no more tears to dry,
   And no more voice to hear you cry.
No more lips and no more you,
   Too young to die. You've left this world.
And now it's my time to cry.

Lennard Clarke
Enfield, Middlesex

ETERNAL LOVE

Tiny voices on the wind,
   small stilled hearts that never sinned.
Our maker breathing on the pain,
   of loved ones left in sad Dunblane.
Their spirits soaring high above,
   transporting warm eternal love,
we search our minds and look in vain,
   but water only comes with rain,
   except for tears, that bathe Dunblane.

John Edward Priest
Leicester

After hearing the awful news
from Dumblane, the words of an
old sixties song wouldn't leave my
head. I use to listen to it as
a child and always found the
words comforting. It was written
after the Buddy Holly plane crash
and was called "Three Stars" I don't
Know who Sung it

"Look up in the sky,
Ours to wonder why.
There are sixteen new stars
brightly shining forth.
They're shining so bright
from heaven above
Primary One we're gonna miss you
Everybody sends their Love."

from a very sad, bewildered
   family in Sandlbach, Cheshire.

INNOCENCE

Innocence in the eyes and tears on the cheek,
  A small and helpless body so fragile and weak,
Unable to speak or whisper its name,
  Why do children suffer this way in such pain,
No-one can ever begin to explain,
  The shortness of life cannot be measured by love,
Only the warmth in your heart is the caring glove,
  So kiss farewell your angel on its journey so free,
A place in Heaven there is surely to be,
  For now time has come to painfully cry,
"I will love you forever - goodnight and bye bye!"

Mr. C. Vessey

KINGDOM OF LOVE

Our hearts they fill with sorrow
  To know that for ones so young
There will be no tomorrow.

Our eyes they fill with tears
  When we think of what has
Happened to those so young in years.

Our thoughts will never comprehend
  Why young lives should come
To such a tragic end.

Our hopes must be of Heaven
  Above, knowing they're safe
In God's Kingdom of Love.

Brenda Docherty
Greenisland, Northern Ireland

Acknowledgements

Thanks to the following for their contributions which made this book possible.

Readers of The Sun.

Fyne Papers Glasgow Ltd.

Montgomery Litho, Glasgow.

A.C.A. Press Cutters, Paisley.

Nextext Composition Ltd., Glasgow.

Opticol Ltd., Glasgow.

Wholesalers including W.H. Smith, John Menzies, Gardners, Bertrams and Heathcote.

The editor and staff of The Sun.

Lang Syne Publishers Ltd., Glasgow.

All booksellers and retailers.